ARTHUR JOHNSON'S SECRET
BLITZ DIARY

ARTHUR JOHNSON'S SECRET

BLITZ DIARY

LIVERPOOL AT WAR

Trinity Mirror Merseyside

Published in Great Britain in 2005 by:
Trinity Mirror Merseyside,
PO Box 48, Old Hall Street,
Liverpool L69 3EB

S.M. Executive Editor: KEN ROGERS
Designer: COLIN SUMPTER

ISBN 0954687191

Printed and finished by Scotprint, Haddington, Scotland

Contents

Foreword

by Arthur Johnson Jnr.

Day after day my father would leave his wife and two young children and set off from his suburban semi for war-torn Liverpool.

Ahead of him was another night collecting the most accurate information he could in a city, parts of which regularly took more of a hammering and saw more deaths than any other place in Britain. Arthur Johnson was the Liverpool Daily Post and Echo "Blitz Reporter".

The journalist, then in his early thirties, would report on the night's bombings for the morning and evening papers of Liverpool, a hugely important city in the war struggle. He knew that those reports would be submitted to the censor and that the truth would almost certainly not appear in the papers – the government policy was that there must be little bad war news for the public.

So when he finally returned home to Morningside, Crosby he would tap out the true story of the terrible massacres and bombings he had seen. He filed his reports in a grey folder entitled "Air Raid Records". The folder was kept locked away as it was totally illegal to keep records of this nature.

Once the bombing of Merseyside had subsided my father volunteered for service and joined the Royal Navy. He was posted to France where he produced a newspaper for his unit. In October 1944 my mother, Stella, received a long and loving letter from him catching up with the news from his camp as the war was coming to a close. Then half an hour after she had opened the letter a telegram boy arrived at the house with a note that carried the shocking news that her husband had died suddenly, one of many to have been hit by dysentery.

Six months later she gave birth to me and named me Arthur. I should have been one of twins, but the other died in the womb.

I went on to be a journalist in Liverpool like both my parents, and now I share with you my father's secret story of the bombing of Merseyside and turn the clock back more than sixty years to tell the tale of the "Merseyside's Secret Blitz Diary".

My mother struggled on her war widow's pension to bring me up along with my sister and brother, Wendy and Michael, who were aged seven and six respectively when their father died. She earned extra money by writing for newspapers and magazines. Money was tight but she ensured her three children had a happy and secure life and went on to be well educated.

As the years went by her standing as a writer grew. She broadcast, her work appeared regularly in major magazines and she had a handful of novels published.

My father had been well-liked by fellow journalists in the city and his colleagues kept a watchful eye on his family, delivering a Christmas tree and presents to our house each year and ensuring that the three of us always attended the exciting Liverpool Press Club Christmas party.

His name is on the Daily Post and Echo War memorial roll of honour. What would he think about his secret diary being published by the papers 60 years after his death?

The typewriter used to write the Blitz Diary is on a shelf in Arthur Johnson Junior's office. As a child he learned to type on it and his mother earned money to bring up her three children by writing short stories, serials and novels on it.

Introduction

Adolf Hitler threw everything he could at Merseyside in the early stages of the Second World War. The region was torn apart, huge areas were flattened, but the one thing the Luftwaffe could not destroy was the spirit of the people.

We were the number one target outside London. Hitler had ordered that the port, with its vital Atlantic links, should be destroyed and he almost succeeded. The death toll here was twice that of any other British port.

The worst was to come in the May Blitz of 1941 when, in just eight nights, 1,453 people were killed in Liverpool and more than 1,000 seriously injured. Fires raged, there was rubble as far as the eye could see, but within three days of the terrible punishment every shift at the docks was working normally.

And throughout these times of nightly black-outs the people themselves were kept in the dark about news of the bombings. Strict censorship resulted in national news reports referring to the raids in the area as being on "North West towns". The people knew the terrible truth because it was right there before their eyes, but it was to be many years before the full details of the extent of the death and destruction was revealed.

Details such as:

• In 14 raids on Liverpool and Bootle alone 3,100 tonnes of high explosives were dropped.

• 3,966 Merseyside civilians were killed between August 1940 and January 1942 and more than 3,000 seriously injured.

• Over the eight days and nights of the May Blitz 100,000 houses were destroyed or damaged on the Liverpool side of the river alone.

• In one week alone 41,000 people in Liverpool had to be found temporary accommodation because their homes had been destroyed.

The courage and spirit of the people of Merseyside was never more evident than during those dark days and nights of May 1941. Night after night, with sickening regularity, came the wall of sirens, then the ominous silence and then the deafening anti-aircraft barrage as the bombs began to drop.

Merseysiders who lived through this nightmare recall the drone of the incoming enemy aircraft. Devastation was everywhere, on the docks, in the city centre and out in the suburbs. Fires burned all over Merseyside and huge parts of our proud city lay in ruins.

It's brutal to recall, but the people of our great port were fighting for their lives and for our future during those dark days. There was also a fear of the unknown. Censorship, enforced by the government for the sake of morale, meant that the newspapers never really painted the true picture of the devastation that was all around. Of course, this could have the reverse effect. Censorship wasn't needed here. You just had to step outside of your front door to have a complete understanding of what was happening.

Liverpool and Bootle took a major hammering, but bombs also dropped in the most unexpected of places with the Germans indiscriminate, or just downright clumsy, in their strategy.

These were the days thousands would head wearily into the air raid shelters as soon as the sirens roared. Of course, many people chose to stay in their houses, putting makeshift beds in the area under staircases that often stood in the middle of buildings and were therefore less vulnerable to shrapnel. It's amazing how many devastated houses you see in photographs with the staircase still intact.

Every night thousands of people would leave the inner city areas for the outskirts of the city where they claimed what shelter they could. Civil Defence workers and wardens were stretched to the limit, but it was the brave firemen of Merseyside who took on some of the most dangerous tasks, not just putting out the fires that that were everywhere, but also helping with buildings that were clearly unsafe.

When the Corn Exchange was razed, the spirit of our people was emphasised when its members simply continued their day-to-day business in the street.

Of course, food was rationed and then people had to be incredibly inventive to make things stretch. Prices were pegged for important foodstuffs or held at reasonable levels by subsidies. The meat ration of 1s.10d a head per week at the end of 1940 was reduced on January 6, 1941 to 1s.6d a head.

One thing that didn't change was the humour of the people. Famous Liverpool boxer Ike Bradley was very nearly a major casualty during the May Blitz. Ike, a taxi driver, had just set down a fare when a bomb fell nearby. His taxi was wrecked, but Ike declared: "I never even took a count!"

It's worth reflecting on the words of the man who was Liverpool's Lord Mayor during the blitz, Alderman Sir Sydney Jones. During a City Council meeting, reported in the Liverpool Echo on May 7th, 1941, he said: "I think I can say without boasting, but with great pride, that Liverpool has stood up enormously well to its task.

"We need steadfastness, courage, foresight, and we are glad to find these qualities prevailing throughout the city.

"We still have that unshaken belief in the ultimate victory. I have been amazed at the way in which our citizens have gone about their lives in the wanton destruction. We shall remember those who have suffered and died.

"We ought to express our gratitude in our sympathy for others to all the members of our staffs and forces who have so nobly come forward and played their part. I feel personally very proud today for the way in which the city has carried on."

The Lord Mayor then moved the following resolution: "That this council desire to place on record its appreciation of the valuable and efficient services rendered by the personnel of all sections of the Civil Defence Organisations of the city and neighbouring local authorities and by voluntary organisations, contractors and others during the recent heavy enemy attacks."

The resolution was agreed with acclamation from everyone present.

If you lived through those dark days, you can feel proud that you stood up for your city. This book is not meant to revive dark memories so much as to highlight the tremendous courage of the Merseyside people. Arthur Johnson's Secret Blitz Diary is something that should be read, not just by our senior citizens who can relate to it, but by everyone with an affection for Liverpool and the Mersey boroughs.

We hope it's a story that never has to be written again.

A NIGHT WITH A 4.5 A.A. BATTERY.
Anti Aircraft Batteries had a very strenuous time throughout the hours of darkness dealing with enemy bombing machines and these pictures, taken in the Western Command, show a battery in operation at night. The gunners are at their stations with a gun in the background firing. Note the huge elongated flash. In the foreground are the men who acted as the predictor and range finder.

The Bootle link

by Arthur Johnson Jnr.

Bootle played a very special part in the story of the war and in the story of my parents.

My mother and father met as young reporters on the Bootle Times and more than 30 years later I spent a couple of years there as a reporter. It was the first weekly paper on Merseyside the Daily Post and Echo had bought and was housed in a wooden building alongside Oriel Road Station.

I well remember starting work there and sitting at what seemed like ancient wooden desks with all sorts of initials carved in them. I'm sure those same desks went back to my parents' days.

My mother always spoke fondly of her times in Bootle and her affection for its people. She also said that the borough took more bombs per square mile than any other place in Britain during the war. She said it with authority and looking back must have based it on information she received from my father.

The town was number one on Hitler's hit list. Its docks received the vital supplies of food, arms and ammunition from America but were also the base for the U-boat hunting pack led by the legendary Captain Johnny Walker. Here was the home base of the Battle of the Atlantic.

My father was the first captain of Bootle Municipal Golf Club and Ack Ack guns were set up on the course. Their pounding of enemy aircraft was so powerful the shock waves bent the metal window frames in nearby houses.

During the constant bombing 80 per cent of the homes in the town were hit. Each night thousands would take to the shelters while others would head north to what was then countryside, many of them sleeping in hedgerows.

This was the front line of Britain's war at home. Entire streets were flattened while ships blazed in the nearby docks. But day after day as the all clear sounded and dawn broke, the people of this proud town would emerge from their shelters or trudge back from the fields and life would go on – until dusk when the bombers would return and the nightly hell would start all over again.

It is important to me that this tribute to Bootle should be included in my father's book. I know he and my Mum would have wanted it.

Arthur Johnson Snr's remarkable personal account of Merseyside at war begins here with his personal diary, reproduced exactly as it was written to highlight the reality of the challenge he faced on a daily basis. It includes all of his rough amendments and you can even see where he has quickly changed his typewriter ribbon mid-page. The roughness of the typing highlights the fact that Johnson was working in a real war situation in which finesse was secondary to getting down the facts.

ABOVE: A bomb dropped in the garden of this lucky house, with no real damage

Summary of First Bombs on Merseyside -- as distinct
as distinct from those on Liverpool.

To <u>Thursaston, Irby and Neston</u> goes the doubtful distinction of be
being the first Merseyside places where bombs were dropped from
enemy aircraft in the Merseyside area. at 2-55a.m on Monday,
<u>29th July, 1940</u> a stick of bombs was scattered over those areas
but all fell in fields and no material damage was done, nor were
there any casualties.

Other districts on the Cheshire side of the Mersey were
"visited" before ever Liverpool felt the weight of the Nazi
attacks.   In the early hours of Friday, <u>9th August, 1940</u> X
-- at three minutes past midnight to be exact -- a servant
girl was killed when Mr Bunney's house in <u>Prenton Lane, Prenton,</u>X
was struck.   Other houses in the same neighbourhood were damag
but this was the only casualty.   The servant girl was in bed
in an attic and the bombs actually dropped before the siren
sounded -- an unfortunate habit they had in the days of the
early raids!   Mr and Mrs Bunney, who were also in bed in a
lower bedroom were covered with debris but were not injured.
The Bunney's home was struck by the third bomb of the series
one of the earlier ones falling in the garden of the chief
officer of the special constables, who was on duty at the
Town Hall at the time .   The second raid in the Birkenhead
area occurred on August 19, when bombs were dropped in fields
at Thingwall and Landican.

Birkenhead's first bombs

In these early raids, <u>Wallasey</u> suffered the heaviest death
roll on the night of the first real "incident" ~~there~~, when
bombs were dropped at Strouds Corner, Cliff Rd, Hill Lane etc.,
thirteen people being killed ~~on this night~~. *This was August
10th, 1940, the date of Wallasey's first bombs.*

17

*ABOVE: The Overhead railway near the
Pier Head after a direct hit.*

Incendiary Bomb

*Filled with highly combustible chemicals, these bombs were dropped in
clusters to start fires. Even those weighing just a couple of pounds could be
the most destructive of all bombs. They were dropped in containers of
different sizes, the average holding 72 incendiaries.*

Liverpool's First Raids -- 17th and 19th August, 1940.

17th August: (Saturday):   There had been many "alerts" in
Liverpool before this date, but this was the first time a bomb
of any description was dropped actually in Liverpool.   Late at
night, somewhere near midnight, residents in the Caryl St area
heard the whistle of bombs which struck the dock road, damaging
the Overhead railway and also hitting one corner of the grain
silo.   The tenements escaped damage.

19th August: The first incendiary bombs to be dropped in Liverpool
fell on this night in the Eaton Rd area of West Derby.   Hundreds
of them could be seen burning in and around the houses there,
although the great majority fell in open spaces of some description
-- gardens, fields or roadways.   The glare as they lay burning
could be seen from the city, a greenish white flickering halo
wxx we were later to come to know so well.   A number of houses
were struck and damaged slightly but no real damage was done to
them or to shops which were also involved.   One struck the
Robert Davies Nursing Home but did little damage, scores of others
falling in the surrounding gardens and fields.

HE Bomb

High Explosive Bomb
A very powerful
explosive that could
damage a large area.
They often had a
delayed-action fuse
that meant they
could penetrate
several floors of a
building before
bursting. This could
make basements and
cellars the worst
places to take shelter
in. Early in the war
50 or 250 kilogram
HE bombs were
common but as time
went on the
proportion of heavier
bombs being
dropped (up to 2500
kilograms) greatly
increased.

Surface Shelter

In March 1940 the government began to build communal shelters
designed to protect around fifty people living in the same area.
Made of brick and concrete they provided protection for those
who did not have a garden shelter. However, within a couple of
months there was a severe shortage of cement, which slowed
down construction.

31st August, 1940.

The Customs House fire.   During the fire enemy planes flew
overhead and machine gunned firemen who were carrying on with
their job.   The Customs House was struck by both H.E. and
incendiaries and while the brigade was at work they came back
and dropped more bombs and machine-gunned the site.   People who
had been attrated by the original fire were injured in these
operations.   Sergt Harold A. Wright, of the Liverpool Fire
Brigade, showed exceptional courage in remaining on the roof
of the burning building, and confining the fire and for his action
was subsequently (on January 23) awarded the George Medal.

At Macsymonds store, only a short distance away, thousands of
tons of food were destroyed by fire.   The Sailors' Home in
Canning Place had a miraculous escape, the building itself
still bearing the marks of machine gun bullets.   A series of
H.E.'s were rained down at Cleveland Square where many people were
injured when a direct hit was scored on a surface shelter.
A warehouse at the corner of North John St also received a direct
hit and was set on fire.

ABOVE: The men of the N.F.S. – known affectionately as the Water Rats – are shown in action on the Mersey. The NFS crews manned the motor fire-boats at the country's ports and their role was to fight fires in the docks and warehouses from the river itself.

Incendiary ridding

Term used to describe dealing with incendiary bombs before they could start a serious fire. It was the duty of firewatchers, who were trained employees and volunteers, to put out small fires and alert the fire brigade. Companies were responsible for supplying employees for fire watching duties.

Liverpool:

        This was the first really seriousnight in Liverpool in
regard to incendiary raiding.   Seen from the roof of the
                building
Daily Post/it looked as if the whole of the dock road south of

Macsymons Stores warehouse to the Herculaneum dock was on fire.

Firemen fighting warehouse blazes from the roofs of tall buildings

could be seen silhouetted against the flames as they leaped hundreds

of feet into the air at the height of the blaze.   In the early

stages of the raid the Liverpool brigade had gone through the

Mersey Tunnelt to assist the Birkenheae brigade, there being

several serious fires on the Cheshire side of the river, but they

had to be recalled later to attend fires on in Liverpool.

Ships were afire in the King's dock, and there were other fires

at the Queen's, Coburg, Brunswick and Wapping docks.   In Tabley

St, a warehouse containing oils and fats was set ablaze, and cotton

was also damaged.   Six warehouses in Shaw's Alley were alight and in

Hurst St another was demolished.   Tobacco stores were involved at

Wapping dock and there were a further two warehouses at Kitchen St

 on fire.   Bibby's linseed stores at Caryl St (right in front of a

big block of tenements) and Sephton St were also gutted and the

grain silo on the dock road badly damaged and burned for weeks .

13 and 17th October, 1940.

LIVERPOOL:

13th Oct:-   Women and children predominated in the casualties when the Myrtle Garden Corporation tenements were struck by two bombs, one at the north and the other at the south end of the block. The bomb which struck the south end of the buildings caused no serious serious casualties but at the other end, whole families were traped beneath the ruins and rescue workers were engaged until daylight endeavouring to release them.   An unknown woman warden did splendid work here encouraging an elderly woman who was trapped beneath a bed on which the whole weight of two flats above had fallen.   Other bombs were dropped in the grounds of the Woolton Orphanage, the Windsor Gardens tenements and Gregorys', Speke.

17th Oct:-   The first of the serious casualty lists from a surface shelter was issued after this raid, many people being trapped and some of them killed when a shelter was demolished by a direct hit in Louisa St.   Many other bombs dropped in the same area, Breckfield Rd, Venmore St, Pagewood St, Brandon St, Beacon Lane and St George's Church, Everton, but there were few other casualties.

AFS - Auxiliary Fire Service

The Liverpool Fire Brigade, the Auxiliary Fire Service and the Liverpool Salvage Corps were in the front line of rescue work during the Blitz. Liverpool Fire Brigade was a police brigade, under the Chief Constable of Liverpool. It had about 250 men, including 50 policemen trained as auxiliary firemen The Auxiliary Fire Service had about 2,000 full-time and over 3,000 part-time firemen. Although short of men and supplies, they were greatly assisted by volunteer fireguards and firewatchers.

18th-30th October, 1940.

LIVERPOOL:

18th Oct;-   Bombs dropped in the vicinity of Fazakerley Sanatorium

for the third time.   Patients in the hospl included soldiers, one

of whom was killed and other patients including children were

evacuated by nurses because of the danger from delayed action

bombs.   This was the major incident of the night, but incendiaries

were dropped in the Lark Lane and Ullet Rd district.

19th October:-   Houses suffered chiefly in this raid, the High

Park St area taking most of the punishment.   A number of people

were injured in houses in Wynnstay Rd and akzNxxxixxxxxxxxxxxxxxx

St Clement's Church was damaged and civilians injured when a bomb

exploded an hour after the plane had gone.   At Norris Green

Crescent a house was damaged and a man named Jackson of Sittington

Rd rescued two people from crumbling house.

22nd Oct:-   Although several bombs were dropped and some houses
                              casualties were few.
damaged in the Empress Rd, near Priory Rd./ Trams were damaged

and one demolished in same area.

27th Oct:-   Three A.F.S men were killed by bomb which dropped at
Queen's Dock.   Pub at the corner of Bridgewater St was damaged. In

& 30th October:- Most unusual raid. So far as could be traced only
one bomb was dropped in Liverpool this night but this, although drop
falling at junction of Thomas St and South Castle St damaged telephon
exchange in South John St.   One or two operators were slightly
injured.

August to October, 1940.

The following places were also struck in the period ~~xxxxxx~~
up to 1st November, 1940, the incidents occurring on unspecified
dates: These are in addition to the places named on the
preceding dates:

LIVERPOOL

Hospitals etc: Southern Hospital, Fazakerley (~~the~~ twice); Isolation
Hospital, Fazakerley; Liverpool Royal Infirmary; ~~Robert~~
~~Davies Nursing Home; Park Nursery~~

Factories and Works: Tate and Lyle's, Love Lane; Silcocks, Gt
Howard St; Palmyra Scent Factory, Aigburth Vale; Enka Silk
Works, Aintree; Braby's, Aintree; Reid's Tin Works,
Fazakerley; African Oil Mills; Aigburth Laundry, Lark Lane;
Brown's Wire Rope Works, Bankhall; Ridley's Laundry, Stanley
Rd; Cobbs Quarry, St Domingo Rd; Liverpool Cartage Co
stables; New St; Goodlass Wall & Co, Seel St; Soho St
brewery; Hughes Bros Garage, Lorenzo Drive; Miller, Rayners
and Heysham Clothing Factory, Lorenzo Drive; Garston L.M.S
timber yard

Warehouses: Stanley Tobacco Warehouse; Wool Warehouse, Gt Howard
St; Leeds St warehouses; Gower St; Dukes Dock; Bacon's
outfitters, Wood St;

Churches etc: Liverpool Cathedral (twice); Mossley Hill Church;
St Margarets, Anfield; Hamlet Free Church, Lark Lane;
Little Sisters of the Poor, Aigburth; St Cuthberts, Everton;
All Saints, Oakfield Rd; Christ Church, Kensington; Welsh
Chapel, Gt Mersey St; Notre Dame Convent, Everton Valley;
St Georges, Everton; St Clements, Maud St; St Silas

ABOVE: The famous TJ Hughes shop in London Road close to the city centre suffered severe damage on September 21, 1940.

ARP – Air Raid Precaution

Air raid precaution measures included providing shelters, distributing gas masks and supervising the 'blackout'. It was the role of ARP wardens to make sure that their local area had these measures in place. They also reported the extent of bomb damage and assessed the need for help from the emergency and rescue services. There were 1.4 million ARP wardens in Britain, most were part time volunteers who had full time day jobs.

August to October, 1940 -- contd.

Public Buildings, tenements, etc: Gildart Gardens, Burlington St;
    Lark Lane branch library; Edge Lane Tram Sheds; Walton
    Gaol (several prisoners killed by heavy slabs of masonry
    beneath which they were crushed); Dingle Mount Tenements;
    Tunnel Ventilating Shaft, George's Dock; Soho St tenements;
    old Seaman's Orphanage (now Censor's dept); Kirkdale Homes

Places of Entertainment: Palace Ice Rink and adjoining billiards
    hall (ice rink three times); Carlton Cinema, Orrell Park;
    Tunnel Cinema (while used as A.R.P. post)

Miscellaneous: Park Lane Goods station; Bankhall siding; Liverpool
    F.C. stand and ground (several occasions); Grosvenor Flats,
    Belvidere Rd; George Hotel, Green Lane (three times H.E. and
    incendiary); Jolly Miller Hotel, West Derby; Gas Offices,
    Duke St; T & J. Hughes store, London Rd; Owen Owens, Reeces,
    Kendalls umbrella shop and Dean and Dawsons, travel agents,
    all in Parker St; Sandon Hotel, Anfield; Hillside Hotel,
    Huyton; Liver Building, Pier Head (clock damaged by flying
    splinters); Journal of Commerce; St George Restaurant,
    Red Cross St; Jack Sands Hotel, South John St; Overhead
    Railway, near south en docks.

Schools: Aigburth Vale High School for Girls; Wirral Grammar
    School, Bebington; Holy Trinity Infants School; Banks Rd
    School, Garston; St Cleopas, Beresford Rd; St Athanasius,
    Fonthill Rd; Morrison School; All Saints School, Anfield;
    School of Domestic Science, Colquitt St.

B O O T L E
    Seeveral docks including Gladstone, Langton, North Hornby,
    Alexandra and the following general places: Bootle General
    Hospital, Derby Rd and the Isolation Hospital, Linacre Lane;
    Bootle Jute Factory;cotton and paper warehouses and timber
    yards;St Pauls Church; Bootle Secondary School for Boys;
    Beach Rd School, Litherland; Alexandra Goods station;
    Costigan's Warehouse, Stanley Rd; Imperial Cinema, Stanley Rd

August to October, 1940 -- contd.

BIRKENHEAD

Aug 7. First Air Raid casualty. Girl killed in Prenton house.

Sept 6. Keilberg Convalescent Home for Children, Noctorum, hit.
About 30 children were accommodated on the ground floor
but although part of the building was wrecked none of the
children was hurt. They were evacuated by volunteers
and A.R.P. wardens.

Sep 26. Incendiaries fell in a railway truck load of bombs but
the load was saved by shunter Norman Tunna who extinguished
incendiaries. He was awarded the George Cross on January
23 and several other awards were made to other men for
this night's work. Other incidents were the destruction
of the Argyle Theatre; P.A.C offices and Income Tax offices
damaged; large store burned and houses damaged in Livingston
St; a bomb fell in road damaging tunnel of Mersey Railway
and service was suspended until Nov 22.

Oct 1. P.A.C. offices again bombed and this time burned, board
room being destroyed. Houses in Henry St and Priory
flats damaged.

Oct 13. Ironmongery store, near large shelter, in Hamilton St
destroyed, also Savoy Cinema roof damaged. Houses in Wm
William St hit.
Oct 18. House in Haldane Ave destroyed.

Nov

August to October, 1940 -- contd.

W A L L A S E Y

Aug 10.　　Stroud's Corner, Upper Brighton; Cliff Rd;　Mill Lane;
　　　　　　Lily Grove etc (13 killed).

Aug 30.　　High School for Girls, Elleray Park etc.

Aug 31.　　Town Hall hit, damage being estimated at £19,000
　　　　　　including damage amounting to £3,500 to the organ.

Sep 5.　　Gandy Belt Works, Seacombe.

Sep 10.　　Rally Centre Moreton.

Sep 22.　　Lily Grove, Seacombe,; Hawthorne Grove etc.

Sep 29.　　Leasowe Rd; Ward's garage; Wallacre Recreation Ground etc.

Oct 11.　　Great Float Hotel.

Oct 14.　　Harrison Drive (1 soldier killed); Earlston Rd Library
　　　　　　Bedford Rd; Withens Lane etc.

Oct 19.　　Coningsby Drive, Liscard (2 killed);　Wallasey Rd;
　　　　　　Tancred Rd; Hazeldeane Ave.

ABOVE: St John's School in Brasenose Road, Bootle was demolished during one enemy raid.

1st November, 1940.

Two short raids on Liverpool. These sirens ended a quiet spell
lasting about three days, the longest raid-free period for several weeks.
No bombs dropped during second raid.

Only incendiaries were dropped in first raid, places struck
including Melias, food dostributors, Love Lane (now a naval storage
depot), Gwladys St School, Walton and Arnott St School. None was
completely burned out.   Four A.F.S. men were slightly injured
at Melias but were not detained in hospital.

WALLASEY: House and shop property damaged.

BOOTLE: St John's C.E. School, Brasenose Rd demolished.
         Houses and shops in Marsh Lane, Jersey St and
         Brasenose Rd damaged or demolished.

5th November, 1940.

A few bombs of small calibre fell in Sandyville

Road and Garfield Rd, Clubmoor but did little damage.

Others fell in Wavertree Mystery rear balloon barrage.

No casualties.

Oil Bombs

A type of incendiary bomb, which contained flammable liquid used with an explosive charge. The idea was to cause some blast damage with the explosive and spray the burning liquid over a large area causing widespread fires. As the Blitz progressed, oil bombs were superseded by a smaller and more intensely burning incendiary made of magnesium.

13th November, 1940.

Several high explosive and incendiary bombs (including oil bombs) dropped during brief raid. Places struck included:

Edge Hill Church (slight damage)

Overton St Post Office   (oil bomb)

Houses in Sidney Place (three houses demolished; people trapped and whole family of about seven people wiped out); Saxony Rd (3 fatalities when domestic surface shelter was hit); and Edinburgh Rd (houses damaged).

BIRKENHEAD

Vyner Road South, Duke St and Price St.

WALLASEY

Claughton Drive and Poulton Gas Works.

19th November, 1940.

Really determined effort at fire raising failed. This
was first occasion on which there were any casualties through
explosive incendiary bombs, about ten people being injured
while dealing with them, including soldiers and police.
High explosive bombs were also dropped. Places hit included:

H.E: Aigburth Vale High School grounds, St Ann's C.E. School, and church /

Aigburth; groundsmen's houses in Everton Cemetery;

houses in Aigburth Rd, Latrigg Rd, Elmar Rd, Wingate Rd

(family of 8 children trapped, some killed), Braunton Rd,

Honiton Rd, Teulon St, (sixteen people trapped in

re-inforced cellar, all escaped; child in next house

blown over rooftops into next road), Priory Rd, Hornsey Rd,

Watford Rd.

Incendiaries: Liverpool College (oil bomb in grounds); the

home of the Lord Mayor, Sir Sydney Jones); Christ Church,

Linnet Lane and on houses in many roads in the south

end of the city. Not one serious fire started.

Land Mine

The Luftwaffe began to drop sea mines by parachute, these were known as land mines. Land mines were huge cylinders eight feet long and two feet wide, which swung silently down by parachute at about 40 mph. They exploded before they hit the ground, causing tremendous damage to surrounding buildings.

Home Guard

The Home Guard (originally called the local Defence Volunteers) was set up in May 1940. Their job was to defend the country in case of invasion and later in the war they crewed anti-aircraft (Ack Ack) rocket batteries. Members were aged between 17 and 65 and mainly in reserved occupations. Approximately 40% were experienced soldiers who had served in the First World War.

28th November, 1940.

In an 8½ hours raid - the most serious to date - land mines were used for the first time on an extensive scale and still another effort was made to start disastrous fires, but again without success, although incendiaries were dropped in all parts of the city.   Whole areas of housing closely populated districts were devastated by the blast of land mines and it was estimated that in a square mile of property in the Picton Rd district alone there were two thousand homeless people when the raid finished just before dawn.   Many of the land mines (at first mistaken for descending parachute troops by A.R.P. workers and Home Guards) were of the delayed action type and these were later dealt with by the mines disposal units of the navy.   One which lodged in the well of the a gasometer at Garston gasworks was particularly troublesome but a Naval officer is creditted with doing a fine piece of work at great risk to himself.   Casualties were heavier than they have ever been -- well over 300 -- largely due to a direct hit on a big communal shelter beneath the old Edgehill Training College, Durning Rd, where about 170 lost their lives.   Many had been bombed out of surface shelter in Botanic Gardens where 2 wr killed

ABOVE: Carolina Mills in Bootle suffered extensive damage when hit by a land mine.

28th November -- contd.

People were amazed at the depth of the craters made by landmines, some of which measured 50ft across and 20ft deep.   At Granby St, for instance, a whole block of shops was just wiped out.

Some of the many places hit included:

> Botanic Gardens (direct hit on shelter, 2 killed);
> Edge Hill Training College, Durning Rd (direct hit on
> building cellars of which housed several hundred people,
> casualties at least 170); Picton Road Gasworks
> (napthalene tanks hit and fired); St Thomas Church and
> many houses in Asfield; Greenheys Rd (bank demolished and
> windows of Princes Park mansions blown in); Rose Hill
> Police ~~sax~~ station; St Anne's Church, Rose Place; St
> Joseph's R.C. schools, Grosvenor St; Adelphi Cinema,
> ~~Christian St~~ Christian St (cinema had bn closed about
> ten days before and was empty); North Gladstone Dock (shed
> demolished); Garston telephone exchange evacuated thro
> unexploded land mine; landmines also did extensive
> damage to houses in many parts of the city among the worst
> spots being Ashfield, Holland St, Granby St, Heygreen Rd,
> and Fernwood Rd. In all, thousands of houses were
> demolished or damaged to some extent.

> INCENDIARIES were dropped in almost every district in the city
> but serious fires were few those at Picton Rd gasworks, a ~~shed~~
> shed at Garston docks and the Highfield Sanatorium being the
> most extensive.

> BOOTLE also suffered considerably through high explosives, land
> mines and incendiaries.   A land mine dropped in Carolina St
> did extensive damage wrecking the Carolina Mills and demolish
> -ing many houses in the area.   Bootle Town Hall suffered
> damage to the roof and windows from blast and houses in
> Trinity Road were demolished.   J.D. Insulation Co and
> Vernons Pools bldgs also damaged.   Other landmines were
> dropped in Seaforth, Litherland, Ford and Crsoby, house
> property being chiefly affected.

In BIRKENHEAD some houses were affected. Casualties light.

additional details for <u>28th November, 1940.</u>

The following buildings were also damaged by land mines:
Olive Mount Children's Hospital; House of Providence, Woolton
Road; St Mary's Church, Sandown Park; Webster Road Council
School;and the home of the Bishop of Liverpool, Bishop's Lodge.
A land mine also fell in the grounds of the Liverpool College,
and another at Aigburth Cricket ground.

In addition Elexcel Works and Mills Distillery, King St
suffered some damage through incendiary bombs.

Lightning Raid
Term used to describe heavy and frequent bombing raids.

29th November, 1940.

In a lightnigg raid on <u>LIVERPOOL</u> which only lasted about twenty minutes, a number of dwellinghouses were struck in Church Ro Road, Robson St and Tapley Place, there being a few casualties. Incendiaries bombs were also dropped at ~~Blax~~ Belmont Rd Hospital and St ~~Maragx~~ Margaret's School, without doing serious damage.

10th December, 1940.

There was no raid this night.   A reliabel estimate of the number of casualties in the city of Liverpool alone since bombing began ꬱ gives the following figures:

Killed	515
Seriously Injured	293
Slight	454

ABOVE: Alexandra Dock ablaze after an air-raid

'Coventrate'

Refers to the infamous bombing of Coventry on 14 November 1940 when 500 German bombers bombarded the city with 500 tons of explosives and nearly 900 incendiary bombs in ten hours.

First Two-Night Blitz   20th December, 1940
                               21st December

          A desperate attempt to "Coventrate" Merseyside was
made on the two successive nights, Friday and Saturday,
20th and 21st December.   First waves of aircraft dropped
dozens of flares followed by thousands of incendiary
bombs and as night wore into morning land mines and high
explosives were scattered.   Whereas in most of the other raids
aircraft had concentrated on the outer districts of the city
on this occasion they made straight for the central shopping
and office districts and the docks, chiefly those to the north
of the Pier Head.   One of the earliest high explosive bombs
dropped on Friday night was that in Copperas Hill which damaged the
Adelphi Hotel extensively and showered glass on people who had been
thrown to the floor in Lime St station by the force of the explsion.
Another dropped in Roe St where a fire engine ran into crater.
About this time the glow of many fires began to light up the
centre of the city, although the most serious were in the dock,
warehouse and timber yard districts towards the north end.
Almost every one of the many timber yards between Sandhills Lane
and Bankhall was ablaze and it was afterwards estimated that in one
of these alone £4,000,000 of hardwood was destroyed.

ABOVE: Great Charlotte Street, looking north, on a Sunday morning in 1941. On the right hand side stands the burned out shell of Liverpool's famous Blacklers Store

20th and 21st December -- contd.

Further north the timber yards and goods stations in the
neighbourhood of Huskisson and Alexandra docks suffered the same
fate, dock sheds also being set alight at the Huskisson.   At the
Gladstone dock the Latex rubber storage tanks were alight for days
afterwards.   At Bankhall sidings there was a great ring of eight
or nine fires one of the fiercest being that of an oil refinery.

One of the greatest tragedies of the night was the destruction/of ^(by fire)
St Nicholas Church -- famous church of generations of sailors
and the nearest church to the Pier Head. Lewis's and Blacklers
stores had their windows wrecked, as did almost every shop in Lime
St, Renshaw St, and Ranelagh St.   Several people sheltering
beneath the arches of the Bentinck St bridge of the Southport
electric line were killed by a direct hit.   Another public
shelter at Athol St, near Rotunda, was hit.   Bombs were dropped
on the electric lines to Southport and Aintree, with the result that
lines were closed on the Liverpool side of ~~Bootle~~ and Kirkdale. ^(Seaforth)
It was chiefly traffic to the north that was disorganised, even
the Overhead Railway near Huskisson dock being badly damaged.

ABOVE: The shell of a Liverpool landmark, the city centre Lewis's building, is a stark reminder of a night of heavy bombing. Just hours earlier the store had been crowded with shoppers.

20th and 21st December — contd.

Among the places hit in LIVERPOOL on DECEMBER 20 were:

Roe St (damage to Victoria Hotel); Copperas Hill (damage
to Adelphi Hotel, cars parked outside hotel wrecked and
damage also done to roof of parcels office at Lime St station);
windows of the Fortress Command, the Press Club and almost
every shop in Lime St broken; Boulton St (windows of Pro-
Cathedral damaged);Reeces depot, Hawke St; damage to windows of
Lewis's, Blacklers' etc ; ~~railway~~ Overhead Railway at
Huskisson Dock, part of station roof hanging over roadway;
Leeds and Liverpool canal burst between Bankhall bridge and
Athol St; three barges wrecked near a large crater in dry bed
of canal, others reared against banks of canal; railway yard
on river side of the canal flooded;impossible to get water
pressure or to get fire float to the north of the break;
sheds in Huskisson dock bombed; Prescot St badly damaged by
mine; shed in Toxteth dock badly damaged by H.E.; Abingdon Rd
School seriously damaged by H.E; ~~Effingham St; Flinders St;~~
warehouses in Effingham St, Flinders St, Rockingham St, Bee Mills,
Bankhall and Grayson Rollos, Derby Rd; Knotty Ash station.

INCENDIARIES:
Some of the most serious fires were those at Samuel Banner & Co,
oil refiners, Sandhills Lane;the following timber yards:
R. Tickle & Son, Denny Mott & Dixon, Thos Rimmer & Co, Slater
Bird & Co, , all on Regent Rd; Edward Challoner, composition
mafrs, Regent Rd; the Sandhills Railway yard;

warehouses at Bankhall Lane and Effingham St;
printing factory in Lancelots Hey; W.H. Smith and Son,
Hornby House; St Nicholas Church, Chapel St;several sheds
at Huskisson Dock; second hand motor yard in Church Rd,
Stanley; garage at 315, Prescot Rd.

Additional H.E.
Extensive damage to Riverside station, glass~~xxxxxxx~~
roof broken, doors and woodwork smashed; Dock Board workshop
at Princes Dock demolished.   Incendiary bombs were dropped
over various parts near the Landing stage but little
actual damage done.

[handwritten margin note:] several killed by direct hit on ?ly bridge at Bentinck Street.

20th and 21st December, 1940 -- contd.

B O O T L E: (20th December)

Many areas in Bootle suffered extensively , particularly those in the dock and timber yards areas, Gladstone and several other docks being hit.   Casualties were numerous and whole districts had to be evacuated because of actual damage or delayed action bombs. In the area between Oxford Rd, Marsh Merton Rd, Balliol Rd and Oriel Rd there was scarcely a house which was inhabited.   A land mine dropped in the garden of the Chief Constable, Mr T. Bell, but failed to explode and the nearby food offices at the County Hall were also badly damaged by fire, and thousands of ration books being destroyed in the blaze.   Some ships in the docks were struck by H.E. or incendiaries, one being scuttled in the dock and crews were evacuated to rest centres.

Places hit in Bootle and District included:
A shelter in Lathom Rd (land mine); St James Church, Chesnut Grove; houses in Holywell St. Shelley St, Peel Rd, Hornby Rd, Southport Rd, Gloucester Rd, Pembroke Rd; Caledonia Mills, Chesnut Grove;in Viola St there was a crater 100 feet wide.
Incendiaries were dropped and caused many fires, one being a slight outbreak at Johnson's Dyeworks.
At Waterloo there were small fires in Kingsway and Middleton Rd.

CHECKING THE DAMAGE: *Claremount Road, Wallasey from where a woman was rescued from this underground shelter.*

20th and 21st Decembe , 1940 -- contd.

BIRKENHEAD also suffered severe damage and many casualties were caused among the civilian population.   One high explosive bomb fell at the corner of Hamilton Square nearest to Hamilton Square station smashing an auxiliary water tank only completed that week and causing a huge crater in the gardens not far from the Cenotaph which escaped serious damage. Splinters slas slashed the Town Hall and a large peice of concrete paving, flung over the Town Hall, crashed into the gallery of the ballroom. Blocks of workingclass houses in Moon St and Bridge St, and middleclass houses in Daffodil Rd and the vicinity of Willner Road were demolished.

WALLASEY suffered its heaviest raid of the war during this period, the total deathroll for the three days of the weekend (Dec 20, 21 and 22) reaching at least 130 although up to that period there had only been about ten fatal casualties. Whole housing areas presented a devastated appearance, the homes of

the people bearing the full brunt of the attack. Roads which suffered particularly were Rowson St, Seabank Rd, King St, Brighton St, Brockley Ave, Withens Lane, Urmson Rd, Manor Rd, Trafalgar Rd, Serpentine Rd, Penkett Rd, Sandrock Rd, Earlston Rd, Woburn Rd, Cliff Rd, Dawlish Rd, Monmouth Rd, Harrison Drive and Wallasey Village.

20th and 21st Dedember, 1940 -- contd.

Even outlying districts like HOYLAKE did not
escape damage on the 20th December several high explosives
falling in fields and on the Royal Liverpool Golf Links and the
Municipal golf links.   Incendiaries also fell at the
Congregational Church at the corner of King's Gap and in
Alderley Rd.

20th and 21st December, 1940 -- contd.

The tactics followed on the Saturday (Dec 21) were almost identical but there seemed, if anything, even more incendiaries which, in the early stages, were aimed at the centre of the city. The raid began within a couple of minutes of the time at which the raiders appeared the previous night. Guided by the fires which were still burning brightly, the raiders concentrated on the shopping and office centres. Buildings which had been shaken the previous night by the blast of parachute mines and other high explosives were now in danger from the fire menace. St George's Hall went up in flames, the Fish Market was gutted, together with the North Market in Cazneau St. Standing on the roof of the Daily Post building as the night wore on, one could see a vast ring of fire. In addition to those mentioned there were the old fires from the night before and their Church Street, where Russell Building and a number of shops were burned out , looked a raging inferno. To the north were several other big fires in the Vauxhall Road area and the skeleton of Holy Cross R.C. Church, Gt Crosshall St showed like black tracery against the flames which were consuming it.

KEEPING AN EYE ON THINGS. *A rooftop spotter and his messenger stand on duty on a mill roof, looking out for any incendiary bombs that may be dropped.*

20th and 21st December, 1940. -- contd.

In many places where there were roof watchers, fires were
prevented from getting a hold but the number of places left
either unwatched or inadequately watched was appalling. For
instance, people on the roofs of nearby buildings saw fire
bombs actually strike the roof of St Georges Hall -- a roof
composed of lead covered timber!   Yet it was some time apparently
before the outbreak was discovered.   There was a similar
case in Whitechapel where bombs were seen to strike roofs by
people on neighbouring property who could not, of course,
expose their own buildings to a similar fate by running down to
street level to notify the authorities.   Being wise after the
event, what was needed was some clearing centre where watchers
whose buildings had not been affected could have reported
the areas in which most of the bombs had fallen.   Sheltering
beneath St George's Hall and for a long time ignorant of the
fact that the building above them was a blazing mass, were
hundreds of people who had to be evacuated to other places
of safety while the guns roared and bombs continued to hurtle
down.   On the other side of St John's Lane the buildings
above another shelter were set afire and hundreds of other
shelterers had to be moved from beneath the Fish Market.

ABOVE: Destruction in Rimrose Road, Bootle

20th and 21st December -- contd.

The premises of Melias, the food distributors in Love Lane,
in wartimex a big naval storage depot, had previously been set
alight but the fire was mastered.   On this occasion, however,
the buildings were very badly damaged.   In the midst of all
this inferno, stretching from the north end docks to the very
centre of the city and even including the Municipal Bldgs,
ix parachute mines and other high explosives began to drop.
Firemen leaving the central station in Hatton Garden to help
fight the Vauxhall Road fires, were lucky to escape death when
a mine dropped at the junction of Hatton Garden, Vauxhall Rd,
Tithebarn St and Gt Crosshall St wrecking several buildings in the
vicinity.   A public shelter was hit in Blackstock St,
Vauxhall Rd, where several people were killed and many
trapped.   Another shelter at St Anthony's Church,
Scotland Rd was hit by a bomb, two priests being killed outright
and others, together with members of their congregation, being
injured.   This was the longest night of the year and the
Luftwaffe made good use of it, for it seemed as though the
stream of planes would never end and while men worked
heroically trying to quell fires or to release trapped people
they were mercilessly machine gunned from the air.

AA Shells – Anti Aircraft Shells
Like other cities Liverpool relied on anti-aircraft guns and searchlights to raise the alarm that bombers were approaching. Intensive anti-aircraft fire kept enemy aircraft at a great height, which made accurate bombing very difficult.

Flares and Tracer Bullets
Used to light up night sky to light up targets and surrounding area.

20th and 21st December, 1940 -- contd.

Eventually, towards morning, even our own guns ceased fire,

or fired in more desultory fashion.   Many lay explanations

were given ; the guns were hot, they were short of ammunition,

our own fighters were up and many even more ingenious

explanation -- but there was never any official statement.

Before the guns did cease fire, however, a number of

civilians had been killed in the streets by the bursts of our

own A.A. shells on the ground.   Just another instance of the

dangers of being lured into the streets to watch the brilliant

show in the sky caused by flares, A.A. shells and tracer

bullets streaming across the sky in lines of orange and

brilliant yellow flame as the ground defences endeavoured to s

shoot out the flares before they could assist the raiders.

        The fire brigade and the A.F.S. worked heroically

on both of these nights and by early Saturday morning there

were 1,200 A.F.S from other districts in the region to help

the city's own forces.   Some extent of the firex damage

can be gathered from the fcat that there were 132 warehouse

fires alone in the two nights!   Unofficial, but usually

reliable sources variously estimated the damage at between

£50,000,000 and £100,000,000. Yet vital transport such as
the docks was not put out of action.

20th and 21st December -- contd.

Places hit in Liverpool on Saturday, December 21, in addition

to those already referred to included:

H. E.
Sparling St warehouseSalisbury St Synagogue, houses in
the Vauxhall Road area, business property in Bridgewater
St,; houses in Madox St, Ellenborough St, Wellington St
Westmoreland Place

Incendiaries:
Many shops in Lord St including numbers 35-91, damaged
in varying degrees; Lovell & Christmas, Williamson St;
Fitzpatrick's and two other fruit traders in Roe St;
two hotels in St Johns Lane and a number of shops (woman
stayed in tobacconist's here giving firemen tea while
building burned above her);Goodlass Walls, and Ayrton Saunders
much commercial property generally in the South John St
and Duke St areas; many shops in the Lime St, Ranelagh St and
London Rd area were threatened (Lewis, for instance had a
staff on duty which threw between twenty and thirty fire
bombs from the roof and found that thxxthx a small fire had
been started on the top floor but they were so quick that
they were able to deal with it before the fire services
arrived); in Church St,Jayes' furniture stores made a
huge blaze which illuminated the sky for miles around;

STANLEY TOBACCO WAREHOUSE NORTH SIDE, BURNED OUT.

Blitzed: Henry Street, Birkenhead

20th and 21st December, 1940 -- contd.

BIRKENHEAD also sustained considerable damage on the
Saturdaynight, several people sheltering in the Ritz
Cinema, Claughton Rd, being killed when a high explosive
bomb dropped in the auditorium, where extensive damage was
caused.   The Laird St motorbus depot was hit by H.E.
and several people in the shelter killed, although thoise
in the nearby canteen escaped unhurt.   Many buses were
xxdamaged.   Many others were killed when blocks of shops
in Church Rd, Higher Tranmere, were demolished, and shops
in Upton Rd, Claughton Village were also demolished. Bombs
also fell in St Aidan's Terrace, near the Theological College,
and blocks of houses in many parts of the town, particularly
the north end were destroyed.   A land mine which fell in
Bidston Hill, near Eleanor Rd damaged many large houses.
Casualties were again fairly heavy this night.

Para Bomb – Parachute Bomb
Landmines and other bombs dropped by parachute.

Several ships were set on fire in the north-end docks. At Bootle the flames burned through a hawser and the ship drifted away from th quay. It was some time before she could be moored again, and only then could the injured men on her be taken off. They were put in an ambulance which was bombed while on the way to the hospl and had to be transferred to another ambulance. This in its turn drove into a newly made crater and the men were eventually wheeled to hospital on a handcart, amid falling bombs and the hiss of falling shrapnel.

On the lighter side is the story of a Liverpool policeman who, after a strenuous night returned home only to find that the road in which he lived was closed to the public owing to an unexploded parachute bomb, and at that time, not even policemenk were allowed through the cordon. Returning to the station, the constable explained to his superiors that he had no clothes but his uniform and asked for permission to enter his house. Rather grudgingly this was given with the strict injunction that he had not to stay ink a minute longer than necessary and that he must avoid all unnecessary noise as these bombs were apt to explode through vibration (incidentally they could also be set off by contact with water, on contact with solid substance, magnetically and, of course, by a delayed action fuse. Charming toys!). Anyway, this policeman, whose family had been evacuated some time, forgot that he had left his dog in the house and of course an enthusiastic terrier barked the house down with delig at the reurn of the master. The con stood there wikkxx frantically trying to quieten the animal. He succeeded but the sagacious dog, having been trained to shut doors, bounced down the hall and slammed the front door, which had purposely been left open. That, thought the constable, was that and commended his soul to his Maker, not for-getting to listen, the while, for the ax awful raor which would project him into eternity. But nothing happened! By now of course he had developed a hearty contempt for German death machines and he calmly collected his clothes, went into the street and asked a A.F.S. man if he would like a bottle of beer. Both returned and when the bottle were opened, the constable asked his companion if he would like to see something interesting. The A.F.S man followed him to the kitchen door which, when opened revealed, a bare six inches away, a lovely shining para bomb, nearly seven feet long. Exit fire-fighter

ABOVE: Total destruction at a house near Merton Road in Bootle.

Additional Details for December 20-21.

shouting "The ------- man's mad.   The ---- man's mad".   So the con had perforce to drink both bottles of beer!

During this raid a Liverpool fireman, who was among the casualties, was brought back into the station with a suspected fracture of the leg and after being given first aid treatment, was awaiting the arrival of an ambulance to take him to hospital.   While he was lying there, a call for still another machine came in but there was no driver available.   Without more ado, the fireman got off his stretcher and before anyone could stop him climbed, with his leg in splints into the driving seat and berated the remainder of the "crew" for being slow-coaches.   A typical incident.

As a matter of record :

    T he canal which was damaged near Athol St during this raid, was not ready for use until early in March.

    The electric line from Exchange station was not restored to use until three months later -- March 24 to be exact.   On April May 1 it was again put out of action by a parachute bomb which dropped at the rear of Bixteth St (see Eight Day Blitz in May for other details).

22nd
~~23rd~~ December, 1940.

LIVERPOOL

For the third night in succession, the sirens began to wail almost at the identical moment the raids of the previous nights had begun. People in the area were justifiably anxious, although prepared to resign themselves to another long and dangerous raid. Fires were still burning fiercely in many parts making what the man in the street regarded as a perfect target for the bombers. Planes were soon heard droning overhead in small squadrons at fairly regular intervals but although there was some gunfire the barrage was nothing like so concentrated ~~ox~~ as on the previous nights. Some bombs were dropped, but for the number of planes passing overhead not in the quantities anticipated from past experience. Then it transpired that Manchester had been ~~xxxx~~ selected as the night's target No 1. As soon as this was apparent, numbers of Manchester's A.F.S. who had been assisting in Liverpool, together with the nearest Lancashire brigades to that city, began the race against time and the East Lancashire Road saw a long procession of fire pumps and buses containing A.F.S. crews streaking back to Manchester.

ABOVE: Bryant and May's matchworks in Linacre Road Bootle with Linacre Mission in the background.

22nd
~~23rd~~   December -- contd.

The actual number of bombs and the damage done in Liverpool
was negligible.Four A.F.S. men were injured when a bomb
demolished the shed at the Huskisson Dock which was used as
and A.F.S. post.   Had the bomb struck the sheds on either
side there would have been a terrific explosion, large
quantities of T N T being stored there at that time.   One
man was killed and some others injured when a bomb struck
a shelter at Rootes No 4 factory.   Some new fires were
begun in the Orwell Rd area and an A.F.S tender going to a
fire fell into a newly made bomb crater. Warehouses in
Forth St, ~~Ensonxxxx~~ Ajax St and Fulton St were struck and
some set on fire, and there was another bad fire at Garlick
Burrell and Edwards', motor engineers, in Ensor St.   An
incendiary also strusk the Commodore Cinema, Bankhall, but the
damage was not extensive.   Also houses in Brock St and Garnett
Ave (H.E.)
            In B O D T L E the Welsh Chapel at the junction of
                                       also
Malta Rd and Marsh Lane was damaged, and/houses at Carolina
and Stanley Rd corner,
St,/and the junction of Markfield Rd and Stanley Rd.

22nd
23rd December, 1940.

B I R K E N H E A D also escaped comparatively lightly
and there were no casualties.   One bomb struck St Werburgh's
Church, Grange Rd and a delayed action bomb fell in the
lavatory of the Cole Street School, but the children were
on holiday.

ABOVE: The Stanley Road Canal bridge where some electric pylons, standing alongside the old Westminster Bank, avoided a hit.

23rd December, 1940.

There was no raid on this night but the full effects
of the previous three days were still to be seen in Liverpool, Bootle
Seaforth and Waterloo. Transport was badly disorganised but in
the north end. Buses bound for Bootle and Crosby had to make a
long detour through Melrose Rd, eventually reaching the docks
via Southport Rd, Bootle, owing to delayed action bombs in the
neighbourhood of the Bankhall bridge which carries the main road
(Stanley Rd). There was a large bomb crater in the same place.
For the same reason there were no trams to and from Seaforth and
Litherland for a period of several days, dockers crowding on to
the buses. In Waterloo the congestion for two or three days was
terrible. Travellers on the electric line from Southport left the
train at Waterloo and then had to walks to Church Rd, Seaforth,
or Claremont Rd, Seaforth. No buses were allowed to run, for
two days, between the Five Lamps (Gt George's Rd) and Claremont Rd,
owing to the number of unexploded land mines in and around the
Rawson Rd area. In the mornings, thousands of people could be
seen making this trek, the scene resembling that of the great
"snow up" of the previous winter when hundreds of thousands of people
walked to work each day. In a couple of days, however, the line was
cleared up to Bankhall and passenegrs wr taken from there by bus to
Liverpool.

23rd ~~21th~~ December, 1940.

Monday

By the ~~Tuesday~~ morning most of the fires had died

down conside rably, there being little fierce glow left in the

sky.   An almost immediate improvement was seen when buildings

in the north end dock area were dynamited to kill the fires.

Soon after the blitz a survey was taken by the Bootle

authorities which showed Bootle to be probably the most bombed

town -- bomb for square yard -- in the country.   It was estimated

that of the 17,000 houses in the town about 8,000 had suffered in

one way or another from enemy action!


```
(                                                    ))
(          C A S U A L T I E S                        )
(                                                     )
(        Later estimates of the casualties were that )
(                                                     )
(        on the whole of Merseyside some 622 people  )
((                                                    )
(        were killed on December 20, 21 and 22, and  )
(                                                     )
(        777 injured. The figures for Liverpool      )
(                                                     )
(        were 354 and 425 and for Wallasey 130 & 185.)
(        These figures do not, of course, include     )
(                                                     )
(        those still missing beneath wreckage.        )
```

ABOVE: Brunswick Street, looking towards the Pier Head, becomes a hole in the ground. The Mersey Tunnel ventilation shaft still stands tall in the background with India Buildings also prominent.

1st January, 1941.

In one of the breiefest raids on record, a high explosive bomb dropped on a tall block of office property in Redcross St, Liverpool.   One man was killed and two others trapped, although a caretaker and his wife managed to escape. Some others were seriously injured, including men who had been fire-watching on neighbouring roofs.   A doctor called to the scene wriggled through the wreckage to administer anaethetic to trapped men, one of whom guided rescuers by calling to them. Rescue workers held on to the doctor's feet in order that he could reach the trapped man.   Two other bombs dropped at Coburg Dock but both went into the water and did little damage although masonry was dislodged from one dock shed and a man seriously injured when it fell.

ABOVE: A traction engine, hidden behind the pillars, during demolition work at the Cook Street arcade

1st January, 1941.

Liverpool Fire Brigade had, up to this time, received many "bouquets" from all parts of the country and from highly placed Government officials on the small incidence of serious fires arising from raids and on the manner in which those fires which did gain a hold were dealt with.   Recognition was given to Chief Officer H.R. Owen, of the Liverpool brigade, for his part in organising the permanent and auxiliary brigades when he was awarded, in the New Year honours, the M.B.E.

9th January, 1941.

Although the was a fairly lengthy raid material damage was

slight and the number of casualties not unduly heavy. The ~~greates~~

greatest number of casualties were at Virgil St (Cazneau St)

where a heavy high explosive ripped out the fronts of several

houses, damaged a cooperage on the other side of the road,

killed some ponies in a stable nearby and damaged the roof of the

Ribble garage in Collinwood St.   Several people were trapped

in the wreckage of the houses and some died before they could

be rescued despite heroic work by wardens   etc.   It was

apparent that efforts were being made to reach each end of the

dock estate, ~~and especialx~~ bombs dropping in the Herculaneum

dock in the south and near the Gladstone dock in the north.

From the number of H.E's and incendiaries ~~it~~ dropped within a

short distance, it was also obvious that one of the main

objectives was the oil installation in the Dingle. Many

houses and other property in the Thirlstane St (Dingle) area

had extensive roof damage but no bomb crater could be found and

it was presumed that one bomb (possibly a parachute mine) had been

exploded in the air.   The staff of Belmont Rd Hospl fought

and extinguished several incendiary bombs.

ABOVE: A gigantic parachute mine landed in the garden
of this Liverpool house. Thankfully it didn't explode.

9th January, 1941.

The outstanding feature of the raid was the lack of success in fire raising. Everywhere people were literally waiting for incendiaries to fall & they were immediately dealt with. At the Corporation flats in Muirhead Ave, for instance, the youth of the neighbourhood was very eager to assist, and did excellent work. One youth, about 16, was killed outright and another blinded in one eye while dealing with explosive incendiaries. Home Guards, returning from drill in the same district, also dealt with many bombs. Greyhounds escaped injury where a bomb demolished kennels at Breck Park track. Places struck by bombs in LIVERPOOL included the following places:

H. E.

King Edward St (warehouse demolished and houses in a court damaged); Mossley Hill Church Vicarage; junction of Broad Lane and Lorenzo Drive (many houses damaged); Blind School, Yew Tree Lane (chapel roof damaged); Virgil St (houses, shops and commercial property damaged; many casualties, some fatal); two bombs in Herculaneum Dock; Alexandra Drive, Dingle (several cas., some fata Chillingham St, Dingle (houses struck; several cas including fatalities); Huyton Telephone Exchange (roof damaged by vey near miss; this is a "caretaker exchange and the girl day operator stayed on duty because the husband of the caretaker was a bedridden invalid and the ××××× exchange was back in service in a very short time)

INCENDIARIES:

The chief incendiary incidents were at the following places: Riffkins (rag merchants) and Sykes' Bakery , both in Rosex Pace; cotton warehouse in Vandies St; Fitzpatrick's garage in Breck Rd; Holt Hall Farm, Huyton (hay ricks) and small incidents in almost every district.

9th January, 1941.

W A L L A S E Y: Four H. E. bombs were at the corner of Albion
St and Atherton St, New Brighton, demolishing a large residence and
killing two people; and at Sandringham Drive, Pennine Rd and
Creekside (docks).

B O O T L E: For the first time in big raids on Merseyside, Bootle
escaped without a single bomb.   Further north, however, H.E. and
incendiaries were dropped, although little damage was done.   A stick
of H.E. bombs fell in Shore Road, missing the alternative targets
of the Gladstone Dock and the A.A. battery at the Potter's Barn site,
Seaforth.   Incendiaries fell in several districts in this area
and a little damage was done to residential estates.

```
(----------------------------------------------------)
(                                                    )
(                 C A S U A L T I E S                )
(                                                    )
(          The total number of deaths in            )
(                                                    )
(          Wallasey since the outbreak of           )
(                                                    )
(          war to the middle of January             )
(                                                    )
(          was thus brought to 152.                 )
(----------------------------------------------------)
```

ABOVE: The night the pub was blown apart. People gather as workmen dig in a deep hole in the road.

9th January, 1940.

B I R K E N H E A D

three
In Clive Rd ~~several~~/people were killed when several

houses were demolished, and two others killed when a detached house

in Golf Links Rd, Prenton was demolished.   The Ritz Cinema,

Claughton Rd was damaged by another bomb together with houses and

shops in various parts of the town including Park Rd North, Thingwall;

Barnston and Argyle St, near the Haymarket.   Unexploded bombs fell

in many other parts, and there were hundreds of incendiaries.

Mid-January, 1941.

There was a long spell of quietness broken only by the sounding of alerts in the evenings of January11, 12, 13, 15 and the early morning of January 16.   On none of these occasions was a bomb dropped on land and the theory that mines were being laid along the coast and in the estuary was borne out by the fact that a day later vessels which had been mined (including a cruiser) began to arrive in the xxxxxxxxxxxx river. One was broughtin lashed between the Vigilant and the Salvor.

An interesting point at this time was the fact that on more than one occasion the authorities were warned to be ready for possible raids on Liverpool.   On the nights that those warnings came through -- long before the sounding of the sirens, and in some cases in the course of the afternoon -- the Midlands and other areas abutting on the North Western Region experienced raids, which pointed possibly to good intelligence work, of which little was heard up to this point in the war.   Even then, few people werex aware of it.

15th February, 1941.

There were two light raids, the first, which began at 7530
lasting only about half an hour.   The second from just
before midnight until 2a.m.   In the first raid apparently
a single machine was concerned and dropped only a few
incendiaries in the Aigburth and Garston districts.
Later there were several planes flying very high.   Some
flares were dropped but there was little H.E. in the city
the Commercial Rd area again suffering.   A garage which
formerly belonged to the G.P.O was struck, there, and a
railway employee was killed.   Several people were injured
when a street shelter in the same area was struck.

ABOVE: Three little girls defiantly wave their Union Jacks in Price Street, New Ferry

24th February, 1941.

                                        near Park Station
BIRKENHEAD: Houses were damaged in Beckwith St/by a bomb

which fell on the embankment close to   Park station.   An

electrictrain standing in the siding was damaged by debris.

Bombs also fell on Bidston Hill.   There were no incendiaries

on this occasion -- and no casualties.

In Liverpool there were no incidents

12th March, 1941.

The "hottest" night on Merseyside since the two-day blitz in
December.   It was, too, the first occasion on which raiders
have been over the district in great numbers on the night of a
full moon -- half moon is Merseyside's favourite season.
Visibility was so perfect that it was possible to stand in Dale
St and watch the progress of a fight between a night fighter and
a raider at a tremendous height.   This bomber and several others
was shot down.   Later it was stated that nine enemy planes were
accounted for in all -- seven by night fighters.   Unofficially
it was stated there were more but the others crashed into the
sea and therefore could not be claimed as they were actually
seen to crash.

The Cheshire side of the river suffered the full fury of the
attack, so it is only fair to begin with that side.   When
daylight came and it was possible to assess the damage to some
extent, people who had been to the Midlands swore Birkenhead and
Wallasey had suffered as badly as did Coventry on the famous night six
when Jerry made his first big wanton attack on the provinces.
Days afterwards there was no indication as to the actual death roll.

12th March -- contd.

<u>Birkenhead</u> :   Land mines, H.E. and incendiaries showered down on B'head and district for hours on end.   This was, in fact, the longest and most severe raid made on any part of the country this year and might be said to have ushered in the "raid season" proper, at least so far as the provinces were concerned. In Bromborough, for instance 41 H.E and three land mines were dropped, in addition to hundreds of incendiaries, and Bebington also suffered extensive damage through H.E.'s.   At Port Sunlight seven H.E. fell at Lever Bros but did little damage.

Wild stories began to circulate as tp the number of casualties, guesses ranging from 500 to 2,000 dead in Birkenhhad alone. At the end of the week it was semi-officially reported that in Birkenhead the dead numbered about 300, with the same number iuziuoiu seriously injured and a further 300 slightly injured. When rumour had done its worst the M.I. released a statement that the dead on Merseyside for the two nights -- March 12 & 13 -- numbered 500, and that a similar number were seriously injured. By that time, of course, nobody believed the statement. Amazing stories of lucky escapes were told. In one case a baby was rescued alive after being buried under debris for three days.

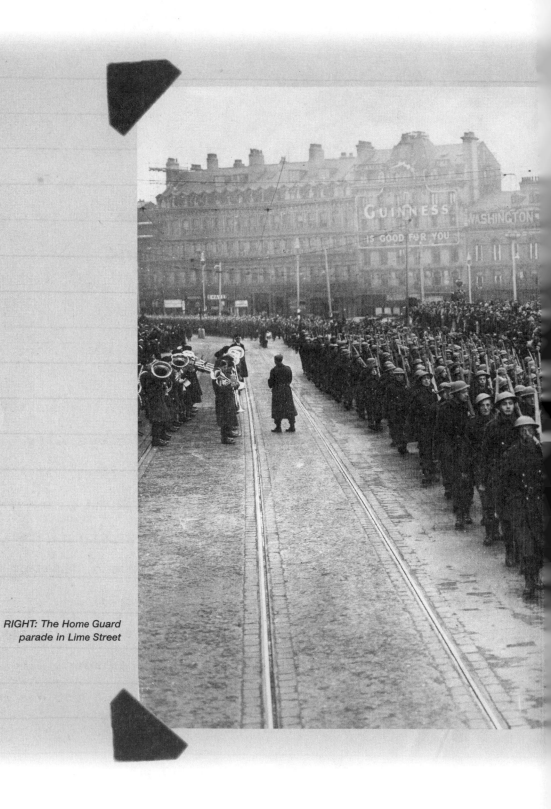

*RIGHT: The Home Guard
parade in Lime Street*

ABOVE: Even Walton Prison did not escape the bombs.

12th March -- contd.

Birkenhead -- contd.

In another house rescuers suddenly came across a girl's hand waving through a small gap in the debris where she had been trapped for fourt full days.   When they shone a light on her she begged them to keep it focussed on her.   She also told them that her mother and father were there with her and that althoug h unconscious she thought they were alive.   She herself had both her legs broken.

The railways on the Cheshire side of the ~~railway~~ river were heavily hit on several places, but perhaps the worst of all was Park Station, Birkenhead, which was almost completely flattened out by a direct hit with a landmine.   The line bwteen P ark station and West Kirby was also hit or damaged by near misses in several places, with the result that traffic was badly disorganised for some days.   For more than a week afterwards, the ferryboats only ran during the daytime.   At first there were buses through the Tunnel.   Amazing to think that there had to be a war before we were allowed variety on Sunday's radio programme and buses through the Mersy Tunnel.   Which is the more sancrosanct?

12th March -- contd.

Birkenhead -- contd

A bare recital of some of the outstanding places damaged in ~~Birk~~

Birkenhead, where between 30 and 40 land mines were dropped, in

addition to 250 H.E., gives, in itself a good indication as to the

extent of the raid.

At the north end of the docks the Vacuum Oil Works was set on
fire and practically destroyed, while one section of ~~Bank~~'s flour
mill ~~was oxexxxxxion~~ burned out, a similar fate befalling Paul
Bros flour mill on the Wallasey side of the docks.   Fire also
damaged the Laird St bus depot when it was hit for the second time
and many buses were destroyed.   Others, which had been moved into
Mallaby St, opposite, were lost when bombs fell on houses in
Mallaby St and P ark Rd North.   The gasometer in L aird St was
also damaged and set on fire.   Some indication of the damage
caused by land mines and explosives is given by the following
incidents: Our Lady's Church badly damaged by bomb which fell on
the presbytery, the rector, Canon J.J. Tallon, his housekeeper
and one of the maids being buried and killed; St Saviour's Church,
Oxton, severely damaged through mine falling on the Caernarvon
Castle Hotel, opposite, where the licensee and one of the staff
were killed;   St Stephen's Hall, Prenton, damaged by bomb;
houses in an estate off Boundary Rd, Bidston, destroyed by mine
dropping on Bidston Hill, which was also set on fire; other areas
in which there was extensive damage to houses were Albert,
Kingsland and Carlton Raods, all in Claughton, Laird St, Borough
Rd, Thornton Rd, Victoria Rd, Bentinck St,   Balls Rd ¥ East,
Oxton Rd, Park Rd South, Conway St, and Norman St, Birkenhead,
while in Clarence Rd, Devonshire Park, between 30 and 40 people
were buried and many killed.

Add Birkenhead blitz --- March 12-13.

          Many people standing in the booking hall of
Birkenhead Park station had amazing escaped when a bomb
dropped through the roof and exploded, wrecking trains standing
in the station.   All the pxzxx people standing on the bridge
on which the booking hall is built escaped injury, although
part of the bridge over the line was blown away.

ABOVE: The Shakespeare Hotel in Sir Thomas Street

12th March -- contd.

Wallasey

Wallasey experienced heavier raiding than it has ever known.   There was no water -- and in some districts no gas or electricity -- for several days.   The water failure was largely due to fractured mains in Leasowe Rd and Grove Rd, the result being that the fire fighting services had great difficulty in getting any pressure on their hoses, mobile "dams" being sent through the Mersey Tunnel by the Liverpool brigade.   Water wagons were toured the borough and some people drew their supply from standpipes on the Promenade, carrying it home in buckets and all manner of containers.   An official warning was issued that all water had to be boiled.   Telephones and railway communications were also seriously interfered with.   Heavy damage was done to property in the following areas:

Warren Drive, Grove Rd, Mere Lane, Claremont Rd, Oarside Ave, Wallasey Village, Leasowe Rd, Green Lane, Astbury Rd, Foxhey Rd, Hillcroft Rd, Poulton Rd, Mostyn St, Palmerston Rd, Erskine Rd, Willoughby Rd, Wallasey Rd, Newton Rd, Daresbury Rd, Manor Rd, Bisley St, Wimbledon St, Lancaster Ave, Field Rd, St George's Park, Church St, Union St, Burnaby St, the Police Buildings, Electric and gas stations, water mains and property in the dock area including mills and an oil works.

12th March -- contd

Liverpool:

The night was not entirely without incident in Liverpool, of course, and for the first time people really believed that there are night fighters operating in this area. There was less volume of gunfire than normally, but the sound of some of the individual guns seemed heavier than those normally in use and it was thought these were the "hush hush" guns of which there had been so many rumours among the public. Spasmodic fire from the ground defence and the sound of aerial machine gun fire suggested good co-operation between the ground and air defences. A running fight between one of our planes and a bomber was seen from the corner of Dale St and Hatton Garden and later it was reported that this raider crashed on the I.CI. sports ground at Widnes. The first stages of the raid were fairly quiet in the centre of the city but by 10p.m -- an hour and a half of the sounding of the siren -- incendiaries were falling thick in the Dale St, Victoria St and Whitechapel area, and along Paradise St and South Castle St, with the result that there were soon three really good fires in this area and some H.E. quickly followed. This was the first time that the military, who first came in to help with fire watching, had been seen in action in Liverpool. They did not create a good impression, except as experts at descending stairs!

12th March -- contd

Liverpool -- contd

One of the earliest spectacles was the fire at the G.P.O.,
Victoria St, where two floors were burned out and others damaged by
fire and water.   Soldiers who were in the city for fire watching
duty were recruited to rescue documents and other ~~suxklyxxxx~~ effects.
The postal sorting departments were evacuated and the mail rescued.
The telephone services who, for obvious reasons, could not be
mentioned in the newspaper reports, had a hectic time.   The
central trunk exchange in the G.P.O. building had to be evacuated
when the top floors were alight. In the central exchange building in
North John St, the exchange staffs had also to be evacuated when a
landmine dropped in the middle of a fire which was burning at
Atherton St, and another delayed action mine dropped close by.
Finally, when trunks had been switched through to the emergency
exchaneg at Lancaster House, and local exchanges were working through
there for a time, too, an H.E. crashed through to the fifth floor
of ~~thexbuilding~~ Lancaster House where it exploded without doing
material damage to the services.   To complete the picture, the
adjoining building, Littlewoods former racing headquarters, but at
that time a N A A F I warehouse, was completely burned out.

ABOVE: A city centre cinema in a picture of chaos as a lady walks through the rubble.

Liverpool -- contd.

Several members of the A.F.S. were killed when a landmine, by
accident or design, dropped in the centre of a fair sized fire in
Atherton St, opening up the surrounding buildings and setting them
on fire with the scattered embers from the original one.   These
were the main fire incidents.   The worst landmine incidents were
at Lace St,(Gt Crosshall St) and St Anne's School, Chatham Place,
Edge Hill.   At Lace St xxxxx tenements of the older type received
a direct hit and scores of families were buried.   To make matters
worse fire broke out among the top debris while rescuers were crawling
beneath shattered walls to rescue trapped and injured.   The
death roll here was particularly heavy and many harrowing stories
were told of the heroism and fortitude of the ordinary working
class people in the most difficult circumstances.   The St Anne's
St School incident was a tragedy in which ten people were killed
including constables (one of whom was never seen again), wardens,
part-time A.F.S and fire watchers. Apparently a landmine penetrated
the roof of the school and did not explode. People were evacuated
from the surface shelters surrounding the school by police and A.R.P.
workers.   A smaller H.E. fell while these people were in the school
and detonated the landmine.

ABOVE: Workmen continue with the clearing up job at Mann Island by the Pier Head, with their own group of interested spectators.

12th March — contd.

Liverpool — contd

The following were the main incidents:

H. E. :   Regent Rd (Overhead Rly damaged); Kinglake St (debris from house on raiwaly line in cutting); University (Engineering Section); Floating Roadway, Pier Head; Stadium (Press seats damaged but not ring); Lancaster House, Old Hall St (bomb penetrated inside bldg and exploded, no damage to telephones); St Anne's School, Chatham Place; office and other property damaged in Atherton St and Stanley St; km tenements damaged in Rose Hill and Lace St; houses damaged in Sessions Rd, Shaw St, Lowther St, Westmoreland St, *Sherlock St, Globe St, Easton Valley,* Upper Milk St; Luton Grove Laundry, Walton.

Incendiaries: Fires were caused in many areas in the centre of the city and it would be impossible to give all incidents, but the following were the most serious;   The G.P.O. Victoria St; Warehouses and printing works in Atherton St area; Littlewoods Bldg, Old Hall St; White Star Bldg; No 2 Court, Dale St police bldgs; Municipal Annexe, Dale St; Athol St Gasworks; A.F.S. Garage, Hatton Garden; St Marys Church, Highfield St; Crosskeys Hotel, Earle St; the Cotton Exchange; The Daily Post bldg had its first incendiary bomb which was tackled before it could do any damage.

13th March, 1941.

LIVERPOOL: Raiders returned to Merseyside at almost the same time for the second night but the raid was comparatively light in Liverpool, where few bombs were dropped.   There were some incendiaries near the centre of the city but none caused fires. Two H.E. fell on the "cast iron" shore at Garston and others at the north end docks but casualities were few and only suffered minor injuries for the most part.   It was evident that an attempt was being made on the river front and during the raid a small tanker, the Ullapool (?) was sunk off the entrance to the Princes Dock, seven survivors being taken to hospital.   Zizixxxx this was probably due to a mine.   The civil defence services were warned that raiders were dropping anti-personnel bombs of small calibre but high fragmentation capable of killing at 50 yards.

In Wxllaxxyz   WALLASEY there w s heavy damage to property including shops at the Capitol Bldgs; Liscard Village; Marks and Spencers Store; Corporation Bus Depot; Water Works; Seabank Rd; King St; Liscard Rd.

13th March — contd.

In BIRKENHEAD the bus depot at Laird St was hit for the third time, one man being killed and several buses destroyed. Two bombs fell in Hamilton Square gardens the damage being chiefly to windows. Houses were also struck in Bridge St, close to Hamilton Sq and also in Mona St, off Alderly Ave, Claughton.

March 12/13 and 13/14.

```
  ( ─────────────────────────────────────────── )
  (                                              )
  (                C A S U A L T I E S           )
  (                                              )
  (        for the two nights were as follow:    )
  (                                              )
  (              Dead        Serious      Slight )
  (  Liverpool    87           74          142   )
  (                                              )
  (  Birkenhead  305          300          300   )
  (                                              )
  (  Wallasey    218          163          161   )
  (                                              )
  (  Bebington    25           50           50   )
  (                                              )
  (  Crosby       16           16           15   )
  (              ────         ────         ────  )
  (                                              )
  (    Totals    651          603          668   )
  (                                              )
  (                                              )
  (  N.B.  It should be noted that in regard to  )
  (        these figures, the M.O.I. stated that )
  (        the totals were about 500 dead and    )
  (        500 serious.   Identical figures were )
  (        published for Clydeside, but there was)
  (        an outcry in the House of Commons and )
  (        in regard to Clydeside more accurate  )
  (        figures were issued  the 500 figure   )
  (        being raised to 1,100 !   (See March ?)
  (        12th, Birkenhead entry).              )
  ( ─────────────────────────────────────────── )
```

ABOVE: Damage to railtrack near Marsh Lane in Bootle.

14th March, 1941.

LIVERPOOL

Merseyside suffered little damage in the third successive night of raiding.   One bomb fell on the railway close to Walton Hospital but there were no casualties and three people were slightly injured when houses in Melrose Rd, Argos Rd and Tees St, Kirkdale, were struck.   There were no fires of importance.

In WALLASEY bombs dropped in Central Park Avenue and Eaton Ave, and at Somerville Schools, but there were no casualties.

After this raid, Merseyside had a raid free period lasting some time.

ABOVE: Hard at work at what was a shelter in Tuebrook

7th April, 1941.

A short , sharp raid in which little material damage was done anywhere in Liverpool.   The outstanding incident was at the convent of the enclosed French religious order/Raparatice Adoration in Edge Lane.   None of the nuns were killed although they and the Mother Superior had remarkable escapes when the convent, and the chapel, were damaged by bombs.   The occupants of the bldgs were in the cellars.   Several bombs dropped on the bldgs and in the grounds of the convent, which was later evacuated. Other bombs were dropped in Orrell Lane, Lilley Rd (Fairfield), Woolton Rd and Edge Lane without causing casualties or doing any serious damage.   Incendiaries also fell in the Old Swan, Wootlon and Soeke districts without doing serious damage.

Other Merseyside districts escaped lightly. There were no fatal casualties at BIRKENHEAD although houses were struck in Town Road, Tranmere and Kylemore Rd, Oxton, twelve people being injured, only three seriously. Bombs just missed the Municipal and General Hospls. Similarly there were no fatalities at WALLASEYwhere bombs fell at Carslake Rd, Erskine St, Vernons Mills, Serpentine Rd, Greenwood Lane, Hawarden Ave, Demesne St, Riverside School, Somerville School, Wallasey Village, Leasowe, Centurion Drive, Meols. Houses damaged at Kingswood Boulev., and Woodcroft Boulev, BROMBOROUGH and also at BEBINGTON and SPITAL.

ABOVE: Bombed railway sidings where a train was literally stopped in its tracks.

7th April -- contd.

Some damage was also done to railways.   A train was
hit on the main Crewe-Manchester line near Crewe, the driver
being killed, the guard injured and another man killed.
Another bomb hit the line at Mollington and damaged a goods
train, but no one was hurt.

Night fighters scored another success this night
a plane being brought down between Lytham St Annes and
Bankes.   One man was captured near the plane and taken
                       at St Annes
to hospl.   Another baled out/and was taken to Seaforth for
questioning.   At Seaforth he sat and chatted quietly while
an army surgeon stitched a bad cut in the palm of his hand.

Apparently this was a night in whcih the
enemy was endeavouring to cover as great an area as possible
with a few planes.

15th April, 1941.

Two extreme districts of Merseyside, Garston and Litherland, suffered fairly heavily in a raid which lasted several hours.   At first it was thought that hits had been made on the airport at Speke but it transpired that all the high explosives and incendiaries dropped in that area had missed the target.   Several factories and

works in the Garston area were hit including Blackwell's
Metalurgical Works, Speke Rd (where thrmite is among the products);
Bryant & May's Garston factory,(where there was a small fire);
J. R awlinson's works, joiners and timber merchants;   Some houses
were also struck in the same area, there being a particularly bad
incident at Saunby St, off Banks Rd, G arston, where several
people were killed and others trapped.   At the north end of
the docks, hits were registered with H.E. on sheds in at least three
branches of the Gladstone dock.   There was a huge fire at the
Litherland Rubber works, which burned for several days.   Workingclass houses a few hundred yards away on the other side of the
canal (in the Webster St area), suffered badly and there were
heavy cas alties there.   Hundreds of people were rendered
homeless through the effaxek effects of landmines.   Other
places hit in Liverpool included Langrove St, Opic St and Arkwright
St.

Bombs were dropped in Wallasey WALLASEY but as most of them dropped on the Leasowe Golf course, there were no casualties.

ABOVE: School kids prepare to be evacuated in Edge Hill watched by anxious parents.

25th   April, 1941.

Landmines and incendiary bombs caused considerable damage
and some casualties in several areas of Liverpool and the
surrounding districts.   Landmines fell in residential
districts including Ballantyne Rd, off Muirhead Ave; at Broadway,
off Townsend Ave; at Glasenby Crescent, West Derby;and at
Pitville Rd, and Mayville Crescent, Mossley Hill.   At Broadway
the mine fell in the roadway uprooting a big stretch of tramlines.
Dr McAlpine's home was almost wrecked by the force of the explsion
but he himself escaped with a shaking, although in bed when the
mine fell.   His assistant, another doctor, who was on the grund
floor of the house was seriously injured and taken to hospl.
The mine which was dropped at Ballantyne Rd landed in the yard
of Roscoe School failed to explode and hundreds of people had to be
evacuated.   Incendiaries dropped in the centre of the city but ża
failed to do any real damage, Lime St station, the Adelphi Hotel,
and Stears St Council school being among the places hit.   There
was some damage to W. Ariel Gray's, tobacconists, in Everton Rd.
Sixty incendiaries fell on X Walton Prison, where the gymnasium
and the roof of the chapel were seriously damaged.   Some
time after this the prison was evacuated.   There was also a
fire at Dam Wood, Croxteth Park, where 100 incendiaries fell in
the undergrowth.

CROSBY and district suffered to some extent, one high explosive
being dropped on a barrage balloon station at Marine Terrace, X
Waterloo, where two members of the Air Force were killed and seven
injured.   The Union Cold Storage bldg at Park Lane, Netherton,
which was then used as a govt food store, was badly damaged by a
bomb.   This is only a short distance from Braby's works, where
depth charges and mines were then being made for the navy!

SOUTHPORT and district was also "visited". The home for Blind
Babies, at Ainsdale was struck by a bomb, three nurses, all young
girls, being killed, and the matron and two other nurses seriously
injured.   The blind babies were taken to Dr Barnardo's Home.
Flames from fires begun in the Pine woods between Formby and
Freshfield which border the Southport electric railway line
lit up the sky for several hours.

There were a few incidents at WALLASEY but no casualties.

ABOVE: More dock drama. The Victoria Monument at the end of Castle
Street can be seen in a central position with the Liver Building top right.

EIGHT DAY BLITZ

1st May, 1941.

What transpired to be the biggest and most concentrated "blitz"
Merseyside has endured began on the night of May ay. Casualties
for this, the first of eight consecutive nights of raiding, were
not heavy but damage was wide-spread, through both fire and high
explosive bombs.   Considerable damage to property was caused in
the Low Hill x area, where several bombs were dropped.   One which
hit the junction of Low Hill and Brunswick Rd did extensive damage
to public houses and shops.   A bank was also wrecked .At Cazneau
St, an area which has suffered greatly in previous raids, house,
shop and business property was widely damaged, but the loss of life
was small.   The North Market, on which the roof was being replaced
after severe damage in the December bltiz, was again struck several
times.   A heavy bomb dropped at the Mile End junction of
Cazneau St made a huge crater which caused traffic to be diverted
for weeks.   One bomb which dropped through the roof of L ime St
station is thought to have exploded on the roof girders beôfre
reaching the platform, but traffic from the station had to be
temporarily suspended because of bombs on the line between there
and Edge Hill.   Other bombs dropped at Bridport St (abt 100yds
from the rear of the Paramount Cinema); in London Rd, & Craven
St, Sxt Kempston St, Stafford St, New Bird St (many people trapped
in houses) Fisher St off Grafton St (again many trapped and
injured); Rachel St; Juvenal Place, Arundel Ave (cows killed when
dairy was struck)Wellington Ave, Garmoyle Rd.   There were
incendiaries in in many districts, the worst fires being at
Crawfords Works in ẕẕg̱ẕẕm̱ Binns Rd and the nitre sheds at
the West Brunswick Dock.

MAY 2 to MAY 8.

(Written May 20).

~~On Friday, May 2, there commenced a week of the most intensive and destructive raiding which Merseyside had yet experienced.~~ Damage on a more serious, widespread and spectacular scale than at any time before was caused, especially to the centre of the city which had hitherto escaped fairly lightly, and casualties during the period were, in Liverpool alone

1232 dead
1341 seriously injured
565 slightly injured

Many huge buildings in the city were completely destroyed by fire, Lewis's stores, India Buildings among them; the building housing Central and Bank telephone exchanges in South John st, was completely demolished and the city was without telephone services, and is likely to remain so for several weeks, if not months. No trams were able to run in the city and it is not thought that the service will be fully resumed for some weeks yet. Owing to the piles of debris and the danger of buildings collapsing, many of the main city streets were closed and road congestion was serious. At one time private cars were forbidden by the police to enter the city. A total of 2,680 troops were drafted into the city to help with demolition and traffic direction. Commander Firebrace, Chief Fire Officer of the country was in charge of the fire fighting operations and brigades from a wide area were rushed to the city. Steel water mains were laid along the surface of a number of roads approaching the Pier Head through which water was pumped from the river.

The most astonishing sight was to be seen from the Queens Memorial in Derby Square, Liverpool's most execrated public moment which remained untouched. Practically the whole of the area bounded by South Castle Street, Canning Place, Paradise St, and Lord Street, was demolished, and the area between Paradise St and Hanover St was almost equally badly hit.

May 2 to 8 contd.

The area between Brunswick st and James st, including
much of the old but extremely ugly Goree was largely
demolished, and Brunswick st itself was blocked for
some weeks by huge steel girders which had fallen
across it. James st station (Mersey Rly) was rendered
unusable and J ames st station(Overhead railway) recd
a direct hit and was demolished, the rail track itself
being brought down to the road.   Direct hits rendered
the LMS (former L and Y) line from Exchange stn unusable
and passengers had to be taken to Bankhall to embark.
Central stn (CLC) was also closed for some days owing
to the fear of Lewis's bldg collapsing.

There was a temporary food shortage at the beginning
of the week and business men could be seen eating their
sandwiches in the streets.   The Queens Messenger
canteens, organised by the Ministry of Food, served many
thousands of meals to homeless people and to demolition
workers and soldiers.   Owing to the absence of trams,
police stopped lorries on the roads out of the city and
loaded them with workers going home.   During the week
there commenced a nightly trek from many of the poorer
districts into the outskirts and country many hundreds
of people journeying by lorry out of the town to return
in the morning.   Fortunately for them and everyone
concerned, the weather throughout the period of the raids
and the succeeding weeks was uniformly fine.

   The G.P.O. on Victoria st was put completely out of
use and business was carried on from the Fruit Exchange
and other adjacent buildings. An appeal by the Lord
Mayor to people to keep out of Liverpool was not allowed
by the Ministry of Information to be published but notices
were erected at stations outside Liverpool asking people
not to travel here except on urgent business.

   On May 14 a mass funeral was held at Anfield cemetery
by leaders of the churches, at which some 1000 people
were buried in a common grave.

ABOVE: Businessmen stand in front of the ruins of the city centre Corn Exchange.

May 2 to 8 contd.

Following the general policy of the Ministry of
Information regarding Merseyside, little news of the
severity of the raiding was issued to the country.
Consequently there were many rumours - that the city
was "finished" and under martial law, that there had
been peace demonstrations, etc. A man was sent to
prison for a month at Manchester for spreading such
rumours, all of which were completely baseless.
It can be added, without "blah", that the oft-invoked
"morale of the people" remained admirable throughout
a really severe and testing week.

FRIDAY MAY 2nd

Just before midnight, in bright moonlight, the
Alert was sounded, and enemy planes were soon over the
city, their work was a foretaste of what was to come.
The Dock Board office was damaged, the Corn Exchange
in Brunswick st burned out and extensive damage done
in South Castle st where tramcars were overturned.
Pitt st was damaged and St.Michael's Church wrecked.
Many houses were demolished in other quarters of the
town and there were many casualties. A house billettg
soldiers in Linnet Lane was hit and five were killed
and 35 seriously injured. At St.Bridgets Church where
300 people were sheltering in the crypt, 10 were killed
and 50 seriously injured. Another shelter containing
80 people was hit in Egerton Road but only one person
was killed.
Church House, Headquarters of the Diocese was
completely burned out and all the diocesan records
were lost. There were fires at South Queens,Coburg
and Wapping Docks; at Sparling st, Bridgewater st,
the former White Star building in James st, the
Gas Co's building in Duke st, the Dock Board Office
and elsewhere.

*ABOVE: Liverpool Museum in Willian Brown Street following
the Blitz on Saturday, May 3rd, 1941.*

May 2 to May 8 contd

SATURDAY MAY 3rd

This was the most destructive night of
all the week and at one time there were so many fires
raging that it seemed impossible to tackle them all.
Lewis's and Blacklers stores were soon in flames.
Evans Sons Lescher and Webb's chemical factory in
Hanover st was a mass of flames. Buildings in Paradise st,Hanover st, Lord st, South John st,South
Castle st, and Victoria Crescent were destroyed.
Blazing fragments entering through the broken windows
caused so many fires in India Buildings that the whole
of the contents and fittings of this huge modern office
building were destroyed, including all the Inland
Revenue (Income Tax) department for L'Fool, the
District Valuer's Office with many thousands of
war damage claims(?) the offices of Alfred Holt & Co,
shipowners,and many others. The General Post Office
in Victoria St was hit for a second time and put out
of commission. The offices of the county court including
the courts themselves, known as Government Buildings,
were burned out. The Museum and Public Library were
destroyed by fire, and the Technical College in
Byrom st and the Art Gallery,together with the Picton
Library had narrow escapes. The Bank and Central
telephone exchanges were burned out; Bluecoat Chambers,
L'Fool's oldest building was practically destroyed.
An ammunition train was hit at Townsend Lane and the
explosion caused great damage.
Other places hit in this long-continued raid
included: Exchange Station, Cheapside Oil and Fat Works,
Bibby's Mills Great Howard St; wool and tobacco warehouses
in Pall Mall and Highfield st: St.Mary's Church,Highfield
st, St.Bridge's School, Walton Parish Church,stables
in Vauxhall road,Salvage Dept,Hatton Garden: Mill
Road Infirmary, which ws badly hit and were several of
t medical staff lost their lives and others includg t
matron were badly injured.

May 2 to 8 contd.

All the premises in the large block fronting Cook
st Arcade were burned out, including the Law Society's
library with 35,000 volumes, many of them considered
irreplaceable. Clubmoor Drive and Lister Drive
were among other areas badly damaged. (See also addition,
which others state data for May 8th)

SUNDAY MAY 4th

        Throughout the day a vast squad of firemen
and demolition workers worked without rest, but
seven fires were still seen to be burning when darkness
came. Soon after midnight another raid started and
thousands of incendiaries were showered on the much
battered city. Fortunately the damage was not on
anything like the scale of the previous two nights.
The Rotunda Theatre in Scotland Road was burned out
and there were fires at Anfield football ground,
St.Sylvester's school off Scotland Road, and
Great George's Square.

MONDAY MAY 5TH

        A more determined raid was made on this
night and further heavy and extensive damage was
done. Much havoc was caused at the district near
the top of Bold st-Berry st. St.Luke's church was
burned out, the spectacle being described by a
reporter from the top of the Daily Post Office as
"magnificent". Shops and works in the vicinity,
including Goodlass Wall's paint factory were also
gutted. The Gas Company's building in Duke St
and buildings in Colquitt st and Bold st destroyed.
Further damage was done to the Cathedral where a small
H.E.bomb entered the roof of the transept. Many
stained glass windows were broken but the building
escaped structural damage.

May 2 to 8 contd.

Great George St Congregational Church was also
burned out. London Road and Islington also
suffered. T.J.Hughes store was badly damaged as
was St.Silas Church, in Pembroke Place, where
the Royal Infirmary also received damage to two
wards. Some damage was done near the landing
stage where the glass from the Pier Head approaches
was shattered. Warehouses in Lancelot's Hey and
a Salvation Army Hostel in Park Lane together with
buildings in Canning Place suffered. The nurses
home of the Children's Hospital was damaged as were
housed in Bedford St and Abercromby Square.

        The Town Hall had all its windows shattered
and the Council chamber made unusable by a bomb
which fell close to, and seriously damaged the
building of the London,Liverpool and Globe Insur
Company. Fortunately no structural damage was
done to the building. "It is a miracle that
nothing worse happened," sd the Lord Mayor who
was in his rooms there the following morning. Many
incendiaries fell in the dock area and there were
fires at Queens and Brunswick Docks, at an L.M.S.
goods yard in Great Howard St,at Flour Mills
in Glasgow St, Several Corporation tenements
were also hit.

TUESDAY MAY 6

        There was another heavy raid on this night
and a great deal of damage was done. The remaining
portion of the Custom House was badly damaged by
fire as was the tramways office in Hatton Garden.
St.Catherine's Church,Abercromby Square, was
destroyed by fire and patients from the Heart
Hospital, nearby were evacuated to the Crofton
Recovery Home, Aigburth.   Threlfall's Brewery
in Johnson St was badly damaged.There were many
fires in the Park Lane area; Wilson's Flour Mills

May 2 to 8   contd

in Park Road was burned and a pipe line at Dingle
Oil Jetty was fractured and fire broke out there
and also at several docks in the South end.
There were several outbreaks in offices at James
St and a hole was made in the landing stage.
In many areas buildings were destroyed and people
trapped beneath them.

WEDNESDAY MAY 7

A further raid on this night accounted
for Morris and Jones's food warehouse in Six
Sir Thomas St being gutted.   A H.E.bomb fell
through the light well of Tower Buildings into
an air raid shelter causing four casualties.
Extensive damage was done to the basement and
upper storeys and Police Sergt Parrington,
famous plunger was killed.
An oil bomb fell in the roadway near the Tunnel
entrance but did not explode.
Other"incidents" took place at Edge Lane where
Sacred Heart Convent and Church were set on
fire; at the British-American Tobacco Company's
warehouse at Commercial Road; in Whitechapel
where five people were trapped under the Shakespeare hotel; in addition there were a great
number of private houses all over the city
demolished by high explosives or burned by
incendiaries.
A parachute mine was found on allotments at
Booker Avenue, the parachute being recovered near
a shelter.

THURSDAY MAY 8th
No bombs were dropped on Liverpool this night.
Enemy raiders were in the vicinity, however, and
a lone plane dropped two bombs on Bootle. No
further bombs had been dropped on L'Pool up
to the date of writing (May 21).

Add SATURDAY, MAY 3rd.

One of the most fearsome incidents, particularly for those living
or working in or near Liverpool's dockland, was the blowing-up
of the ammunition ship ss Malakand (Brocklebank Line) in the
Huskisson Dock, Liverpool, a few hours after the "all-clear" had
sent people gratefully to their beds.   There was scarcely a soul on
Merseyside who did not awaken to the shock of the tremendous
detonation. The Malakand, laden with ammunition and almost ready
for sea, was tied up at the Huskisson alongside another ship.   In
temporary command of both was Capt Howard Cooke Kinley, aged 43, of
169, Queen's Drive, on duty as a shore relief master.   For the
galantry he showed in the subsequent events he was commended for
bravery (London Gazette and D.P., Sept 10, 1941).   The awful
succession of events leading up to the explosion began when a
wayward barrage balloon became entangled in the ships rigging and
ignited. Almost immediately showers of incendiary bombs descended on
the luckless ones engaged in clearing the obstruction.   Many of the
bombs fell into the dock, others dropped into the sheds all around
and some burned fiercely on the deck and upperworks of the ammunition
ship.   In a surprisingly short space of time it appeared as though
three sides of the dock were ablaze.   Capt Kinley, shouldering the
what was probably the greatest responsibility on the dock estate at
that moment, concentrated his attention on the fire aboard the
Malakand.   He evacuated Lascar seamen and with the assistance of
a chief officer, some gunners and a coloured leading seman got one
ship away from the scene and fought the fire.   Those flying
above also concentrated their attention on such a welcome target,
as was shown by the H.E. bombs which fell on and near the blazing
sheds.   Realising the need for expert help, Capt Kinley commandeered
a car and drove off through a lane of burning sheds in search of
fire fighters and pumps.   It was not an easy matter to find the
help he required.   Firemen were at a premium and when Capt Kinley
returned to his charge the position seemed well nigh hopeless.The
top floors of the sheds were burning like beacons. The fire on the
Malakand had gained a strong hold.   The only hope was to scuttle the
ship.   The all clear was sounded and while the rest of the city went
to bed the serious business of tackling the danger in the Huskisson
Dock was continued unremittingly.

ABOVE: The collapsed wreckage of the overhead railway

ADD SATURDAY, MAY 3rd -- 2.

The ship's moorings had been cast off and the Malakand was
manhandled as far as possible off the quay while water was from
hoses was poured into the smk smoking smouldering structure above
the waterline.   At one time it was thought there was a chance the
fire would be beate and that the danger below decks would be averted.
But this as not to be. Without warning the cargo of high explosives
blew up.Capt Kinley was on the quayside scarcely a hundred x yards
away at the time.   He felt the searing blast of the explosion and was
thrown against the side of a shed.   Pieces of debris struck him,
inflicting head and leg wounds.   Others nearer, and even some who
were further away didi not live through the experience and it is Capt
Kinley's opinion that he was standing in the "vacuum" and that the
blast passed over his head.   Some idea of the force of the
explosion can be gained from the knowledge that parts of the ship's
steel plates were recovered two and a half miles away inside the
city itself!   The stoutly built dock sheds were demolished as
though trampled under some giant foot.   The Overhead railway and
station at the dock entrance were twisted out of shape; dock walls
many feetthick were crumbled to dust, and in the middle of the dock
the remains of the Malakand, a shattered hulk lying on her side like
some agonised whxxdx whale could be seen for many a week afterwards.
Policemen, firemen, dock workers lost their lives in the disaster
but a number of those who survived the ordeal gained official notice
for galdantry in the face of extreme danger.

       A big "incident" such as this provides many freakish
examples of the extent to which people become inured to bombing.
Two x engineers who had been working on the ship and were standing
by helping to fight the fire went, after the all-clear to the lavatory
As they passed under the Overhead -- truly the dockers umbrella in
this case -- they heard the explosion and, seeing ships plates flying
through the air flung themselves flat on the ground.   When they
raxbuxiaxd rose cautiously to their feet one looked at the other and
said "I've lost me bloomin' hat.   No I've not, you have got it on
Wally."   "Well I'm damned," retorted Wally. "Where the ----'s
mine then?"   Wally never found his hat, which annoyed him much
more than the dozens of bruises he suffered from flying debris or
the shock he received when a ship's plate tore a huge hole in the
railway not far away.

ABOVE: The roof of a Liverpool tram lies in the middle of a devastated street.

MAY 2 to 8   contd

DAMAGE IN THE DISTRICTS

During this period, which was one
of bright moonlight, the city of Liverpool
obviously the principal objective of the raiders,
but despite the damage done to it and the attention
it received, the other Merseyside boroughs did not
escape their share of attention.

BOOTLE

This borough was again badly damaged.
The main shopping street of the town was described
as being "absolutely unrecognisable" and several
churches were badly damaged. The Town Hall was
damaged and other Corporation departments situated
outside it completely gutted. Severe damage was
done to Langton, Gladstone and Alexandra Docks
were ships were sunk; to Harland and Wolff's
ship repairing works; Johnson's Dye Works,
Bryant and May's match factory, Scott's bakery
and other works. The Metropole theatre and the
Boy's Secondary School were completely burnt out.

WALLASEY   Much damage was again done to residientia
property here. Three bombs fell on the promenade
near the bathing pool; the Royal Daffodil 11,
moored at Seacombe Ferry, was hit and sunk,
seven men aboard her escaping uninjured.
A land mine fell on the Rake Lane Cricket Ground
doing great damage to surrounding houses. A bomb
fell on Bidston Golf Course but did not explode.

MAY 2 to MAY 8

BIRKENHEAD.

Many houses in the town were demolished during the week. Woodchurch Road large Council School was almost completely destroyed. Fire almost destroyed the old ironworks at Cammell Lairds and damaged the old Priory chapel. The Hermitage, formerly the residence of Rheinhardt , the German consul who was suddenly recalled shortly before the war, was demolished. The general opinion was that Rheinhardt should have been in it at the time. The occupants were injured. Two members of the police force and a bus driver were killed by an anti-aircraft shell, and one of these missiles also pierced a house at West Kirby.

DAILY POST 11/10/41.
DATE OF INCIDENT — MAY 3rd AT
ALEXANDRA DOCK.

CLEARED BLAZING DOCK-SHED OF EXPLOSIVES

LIVERPOOL POLICE OFFICERS' HEROIC WORK RECOGNISED

Liverpool police officers who, during a concentrated bombing raid on the city, faced death on the dock area in a desperate race against time to remove quantities of ammunition and Army stores from a dock-shed which was on fire at one end, and others who carried wounded through a blazing dock-shed, figure in the latest list of decorations for civil defenders, announced in last night's *London Gazette*.

George medals are awarded to Constable Percy Albert Jones Green, aged 38, of 60 Parthenon Road, Liverpool, and Constable Frederick Albert Spicer, aged 40, of 302 Walton Hall Avenue, Liverpool, who took a leading part in the removal of the explosive material. Both are married with seventeen years' service, respectively, in the Liverpool Police Force.

Inspector's Bar To B.E.M.

Inspector T. M. Skelton, aged 39, of 54 Parkhurst Road, Liverpool, who was awarded the British Empire Medal in February last for the assistance he gave in the rescue of a family from a blazing

from wire mattresses, and the injured men were carried through a blazing dock-shed.

CROSBY AND BOOTLE
MEDALS FOR CIVILIANS AND POLICE

"It was a sticky piece of work," said Mr. Arthur Lewis Cochrane, Superintendent of Crosby Civil Defence Rescue Service, describing the rescue of a Crosby woman from under the ruins of her home, for which he and Mr. George Allen, full-time rescue-squad worker, of 38 Granville Road, Seaforth, have each been awarded the British Empire Medal. Mr. Cochrane, whose home is 3 Hastings Road, Crosby, has already received a commendation for his work during previous raids on the borough. During one of the worst nights of a heavy blitz Mr. Cochrane and Mr. Allen were working in the glare from a burning gas main when they heard a faint call for help from the ruins of a house. Mrs. Joyce Barry, they discovered, was buried under the debris.

Mr. Cochrane followed Mr. Allen and found him in a very dangerous position, for the woman was pinned below and a beam was cutting into Mr. Allen's spine as he worked to release her. "With my foot," said Mr. Cochrane. "I managed to lift a pillow from the debris round her and tucked it between the timber joists and Allen's spine." The two men then managed to hold up the wall with their backs, and Mr. Cochrane lifted Mrs. Barry's head clear, cupping it in his hand and thus enabling her to breathe. They were working for an hour and ten minutes before they managed to ease her out inch by inch after morphia had been administered by a doctor.

Dug In Debris With Bare Hands

Constable William H. Cottier, of 187 Southport Road, Bootle, a clerk in the office of the Chief Constable of Bootle, has been awarded the British Empire Medal for his rescue of a man, the only survivor, from a blazing house.

P.C. GREEN (G.M.)   P.C. SPICER (G.M.)

P.C. GREEN
(G.M.)

P.C. SPICER
(G.M.)

cellar, receives a bar to the British Empire Medal, for daring fire again to rescue the injured. He formed a stretcher party and carried wounded sailors to safety through the only route available—a blazing dock-shed. Constables H. Gannaway and S. J. Gardler, who shared the danger, receive British Empire Medals. One Bootle police officer and two Crosby civil defence workers also receive the British Empire Medal.

The George Medallists, Constables Green and Spicer, found themselves suddenly confronted with a most dangerous situation. Fire broke out in a shed which contained a cargo of Army stores including ammunition. Moored alongside the quay was a motor ship loaded with a similar cargo and immediately outside the burning shed were railway trucks also containing ammunition.

Complicating the situation was the presence of kerosene. The fire spread rapidly towards the inflammable stores. The two constables first warned the master of the ammunition ship to move his charge to a place of safety. This was done, the constables casting off the ropes. Then, using an electric bogey, they commenced the race against time, and, by man-handling equipment and explosives, succeeded in clearing a large quantity of material before help arrived.

A number of other Liverpool police officers, in charge of Inspector Skelton, formed the relief party, and together the task of shunting waggons, hauling loads, and clearing the explosives from the path of the fire was carried through. The official citation makes it clear that during this time the area was a constant target for enemy bombers and burning debris fell all around the workers. Officers of the relief party who have been officially commended for bravery are: Sergeant C. F. Blackburn, Sergeant A. Watson, and Constables R. H. Metcalfe, T. Roughley, and W. A. Young.

Rescue Dash Through Fire

Inspector Skelton was called within the hour to a bombed ship which had caught fire. Two members of the crew lay injured and helpless aboard the burning ship. Mr. George Ernest Wheeler, an able seaman, of Swansea, who is awarded the George Medal, volunteered to board the ship and attempt a rescue. He fastened a rope to one of the injured crew and lowered him over the side, where he was hauled ashore by Inspector Skelton and his co-medallists, Constables Harry Gannaway, aged 38, of 21 Culme Road, Liverpool, and War-Reserve Constable Sidney John Gardler, a former fruit porter, of 21 Sandyville Road, Liverpool.

After a naval officer had also climbed aboard to assist, Wheeler got the second casualty safely to the quay, where Inspector Skelton improvised stretchers

Dug In Debris With Bare Hands

Constable William H. Cottier, of 187 Southport Road, Bootle, a clerk in the office of the Chief Constable of Bootle, has been awarded the British Empire Medal for his rescue of a man, the only survivor, from a blazing house. Constable T. J. McCarthy, of 38 Oxford Road, Bootle, who already holds the George Medal for previous gallantry in a raid; War Reserve Constable James Besford, of 464 Southport Road, Bootle; and Special Constable Stanley Percival Jones, 470 Hawthorne Road, Bootle; each receive a commendation for their bravery in the same rescue, Besford being the first War Reserve constable in the borough to receive official recognition.

"It was just fortunate that we were passing and the job had to be done," said Constable Cottier to the *Daily Post*, "and had it not been for the help of

INSPECTOR T. M. SKELTON
(Bar to B.E.M.)

P.C. GANNAWAY
(B.E.M.)

Special Constable Jones and War Reserve Constable Besford, this rescue could never have been carried out, for it was essentially a job for team work." Constable McCarthy, a member of the motor patrol, picked up the other officers, and as they came along a main road a huge sheet of flame shot into the air from a house which had a direct hit. They climbed over the debris and Cottier scooped a hole in some of the wreckage, saying that he had heard a cry from underneath. The flames were creeping nearer and the heat was intense, but Cottier kept digging away with his bare hands, and soon made a hole.

A huge beam, however, partly blocked the way and with Cottier using his body as a fulcrum they gradually managed to move the beam. One of the men said: "It was only through Cottier's physical strength and endurance that it could be done. The flames were at one time within inches of his body."

Commendations for bravery in connection with rescue work at the Mill Road Infirmary are also made to Sergeant J. Carson, Constable N. Morrisey, and War Reserve Constable D. C. Lewis, of the Liverpool Police Force.

28th May , 1941.

New methodsx of ground defence were tried onxthixnixkk during this raid, shells with a multiple burst being used. What a row! It seemed as if everything but the Liver clock was thrown at the few raiders which were over and once, when a raider was apparently caught in a perfect cone of searchlights, the sky and streets were brilliantly illuminated by the flash of guns and bursting shells. Unfortunately all of the shells did not burst in the air and the only damage done in Liverpool was by "dud" AA shells exploding after dropping among houses. Such incidents were reported at Dove St, Beaumont St, Can St, Carrington St, Granby St (all in the Lodge Lane area), Normanby St, Longmoor Lane and Utting Ave, where an Anderson shelter stood up to a direct hit with a shell. A youth was killed at Dove St and in various areas there were six serious casualties.

A raider was shot down by a night fighter at Buckley, Mold, and all its bombs exploded. One German airman landed in the yard of a police station and another is believed to have surrendered to a farmer.

A number of people were trapped when bombs were dropped in Bootle, Litherland and Crosby. Others did some damage at Neston and Upton, Birkenhead. One bomb which fell in Manor Drive, Upton, Hemolished two houses and three people all over 70 were rescued by wardens. Other bombs fell in fields. There were no casualties.

ABOVE: Houses damaged in Bebington after a "Tip and Run" raid by the Luftwaffe.

30th May, 1941.

There was again heavy gunfire in Liverpool, but little damage in city, the only bomb dropped in Liverpool being at the junction of Pinehurst Ave and Townsend Lane, where a crater was caused in a garden and two houses were damaged.   There were no casualties. Some indendiaries were also dropped in isolated districts but did little damage.   The dock area was again the centre of one fire raising effort, but this met with little success, small fires at the N.W. Toxteth, E Brunswick and Coburg docks being quickly under control.

As examples of the extra work thrown on the authorities by innocent or malicious persons two incidents can be quoted. In the first some young people acted in quite good faith in reporting to a bafrage balloon site that they had seen a man acting very suspic- iously.   Men from the site went to the spot indicated and saw a man carrying over his shuolder what they took to be a white crash helmet (visions of parachutists or German pilots!).   When challenged he ran away and it took the police some hours to establish that he was a friendly foreign sailor with a white painted steel helmet   He thought he was shouted at for being away from his ship in an air raid.
The other incident remains a mystery.   After a heavy bombardment somebody reported that three people in an Anderson shelter had been covered with a phospherous matter which left behind it brown stains and a burning sensation.   More investigation which yielded no clue as to the origin of the story.

31st May, 1941.

~~zksnzxxxxdxt~~

Again Liverpool escaped serious damage in a raid which produced spells of very heavy gunfire and planes could be heard passing overhead frequently.   There was one instance of damage to house property but the greatest damage was done at the north end docks, particularly the Gladstone and Hornby docks, where several sheds were struck and quaysides damaged.   One of the few timber yards left in Bootle was also damaged.

Waterloo and Crosby suffered more extensively, there being a fairly heavy death roll ak in the Brook Vale area (Brookside and Brookfield Aves) where a landmine dropped.   This area had been damaged by bombs in previous raids but this was the heaviest blow so far and Anderson shelters were in some cases lifted clean out of the ground.   ~~Among the casualties was the father of Mary Hagen, a Waterloo schoolgirl, whose murder in a blockhouse by a soldier had horrified the district a few months before.~~   The windows of the Waterloo telephone exchange were blasted out and the operqtors had to go to an emergency board for a time because of light showing through the windows.   Even after they returned they had to work the ordinary board by the light of shaded hand torches, Other houses in Norway St, Waterloo, and Church Rd, Seaforth, were damaged and traffic was diverted for several days through bombs which fell in and close to the main raod, Crosby Rd South.   Cows were killed when a dairy was struck in Somerville Rd, and ~~zxik~~ traffic ~~vxx~~ on the electric line was ~~fox~~ dislocated for a day by a bomb from the same plane which damaged the track slightly near St John's Rd level crossing.

Several people were killed and others buried in debris when bombs fell on shops in Heswall Lower Village.   Others were dropped in T elegraph Rd, Heswall, opposite the Children's Hospl.

There were about this time many other occasions when the sirens x sounded and there was gunfire but no other incidents in Liverpool. Raiders were obviously going elsewhere. Manchester being the "appointed place" on the night of June 1st.

ABOVE: Air Raid damage near Hatton Garden.

24th June, 1941.

Birkenhead suffered more than Liverpool in a raid lasting only two
hours on one of the shortest nights in the year -- apparently a ɛɡɛɪʐɪɴɪ
"gesture" raid.   About sixty houses were severely damaged in
Westdale and Southdale Rds, Higher Tranmere, and Allcott Ave, Hr
Tranmere Tranmere, a number of people being trapped in the debris.
Six people were killed and there were a number of other casualties.
Incendiaries started a number o fires in the town area, a paint
shop and a laundry suffering damage in Cleveland St.   A determined
attack was made on the Rendel St entrance to the Mersey Tunnel, debris
from one H.E. blocking that entrance completely for a time, but
within a short time one lane was opened for traffic and by noon both ʙ
lanes were cleared.   Another bomb dropped on a stable close to the
entrance to the Tunnel.   Five horses were killed and nine rescued.
A fire watcher was killed here.

Another plane flying exceptionally low dropped a bomb near the L'pool
Princes dock, a goods train in the dock avenue being struck.   Apart
from a   few incendiaries there were few other incidents in Liverpool.

In Wallasey a thousand poynds bomb demolished Holland House, Seabank
Road, ʆɒʀɴɪʐʀ formerly a maternity home, but now evacuated.   ʂʙ
Surrounding propeety was also damaged.   Other bombs fell in Dalton
Rd and Dalnorton Rd, New Brighton, and in Gorsedale Rd and Oakdale
Rd, Seacombe, but there were no casualties from any of these
incidents.

BIRKENHEAD Raid Damage to end of JUNE,1941.

Between 9th August amdx 1940 and 26th June, 1941the number of houses
damaged by enemy action in the birkenhead area reached the total of
19,296.   Of these, 540 have been totally destroyed, 1587 seriously
damaged and marked for demolition, 1634 seriously damaged but
capable of repair and still habitable, 4101 seriously damaged and
capable of repair but from which the inhabitants have been evacuated
and 13,561 slightly damaged -- excluding those where only window glass
was broken.   Counting those houses damaged on more than one occasion
-- some have been damaged in three seaparate raids -- the total
is 20,976.   First aid external repairs have been earried out to
15,975 houses and extended first aid repairs internally are being xaxx
carried out in 280 privately-owned houses and 260 Corporation houses.
There have been 256 Corporation houses have been used for re-housing
and 182 houses have been requisitioned, of which 136 are now occupied.

ABOVE: Mr and Mrs Clague return to their flattened property although their Anderson Shelter had a remarkable escape.

23rd July, 1941.

A particularly heavy barrage -- evidently a first try-out for the
"hush-hush" A.A. devices which had been freely hinted at by all the
relatives of men who come down with to work on a tram on which the
conductor has a boy who has a friend whose second cousin is in the
A.A. -- greeted the few raiders who visited Merseyside on this
night.   Few bombs were dropped.   In Liverpool there was no
damage by enemy action, but two men were injured by dud ack ack
shells exploding when they hit the ground.

Heavy calibre bombs were dropped in Birkenhead where there were eight
fatal casualties. One more bomb fell a feet from a gasometer at the
gas works near Central Station, falling just inside the railway
sidings.   The Duke St and Cleveland St areas, already badly blitzed,
were again bombed.   Brick surface shelters collapsed through the blast
of bombs dropped in Arthur St, the walls of the shelters being blown
out and the occupants of the shelters trapped when the heavy concrete
roofs of the shelters fell in.   Only a few days previously the
bridge over Park Station had been reopened after being reconstructed
as a result of damage sustained on the night of March 12/13.   Once
again direct traffic along Duke St to and from Wallasey had to be
diverted.   A short distance from the bridge a bomb fell on the
concrete roadway and huge slabs of concrete were hurled into
the air striking the roadway again with such force that sections
of the road folded back like the leaves of a book.

At Hoylake a few bombs fell on the foreshore and into the
sea, causing neither damage nor casualties.

Three men received slight injuries when a bomb damaged two
houses at Birkdale.   Another bomb fellinto a builders' yard.

Three other bombs fell in a cluster not far from a big gun
site at For Crosby, narrowly missing A.T.S. and army huts.

ABOVE: Bomb damage in Rimrock Street, Bootle.

MONTH OF OCTOBER, 1941.

Merseyside enjoyed -- and "enjoyed" is the right word! -- a longer raid-free spell than many people expected during the summer and early autumn months, for it was not until the middle of October that the banshee began to wail fairly consistently between 8p.m and 9p.m. On many occasions there were no incidents locally and even when bombs were dropped raids usually ended by midnight.

OCTOBER 12: The official phraseology "small scale activity" describes this and the other raids during the month quite well. One raider was destroyed. H.E. dropped on an Ormskirk farm killing livestock and poultry and damaging farm buildings, but there were no casualties. Other bombs dropped in fields near Blue Bell Lane, Huyton, but did little damage. Four others, which came down in a bunch, failed to explode when they dropped in the Brownmoor Lane-Northern Rd area of Crosby and although people had to be evacuated there were no casualties.

OCTOBER 20: Once again poor old Bootle took the brunt of the attack. One of the big holders at the Linacre Gasworks was struck by a direct hit. A hundred yards away/paramines a dropped in Surrey St doing considerable damage to houses there and in Worcester Rd, and Gloucester Rd etc. The Mayor of Bootle , Cclr J.S. Kelly, was among those who helped in the rescue work, encouraging rescue squads and solacing trapped people to whom he talked. At least 14 were killed & 50 injured here.

MONTH OF OCTOBER -- CONTD.

20th October (cntd):   Birkenhead also suffered, one heavy H.E. being dropped at the rear of Beryl Rd, Upton, not far from Upton station. The bomb, a paramine, fell on to a market garden, but the explosion caused extensive damage to property in the neighbourhood.There were no fatal injuries, but about five people were slightly injured.

OCTOBER 22:   This was almost a duplicate of the raid two days earlier, watchers in Liverpool being able to trace the wall of fire sent up by the A.A defences in what might be called the outer perimeter of the port's defences, which are some miles away. An almost complete circle of gunfire could be seen round the city, running from the Widnes and Warrington area in the south, through Cheshire and North Wales, and up to the Crosby and other northern points.   Adding to the spectacular side of the show was the Aurora Borealis, the pale glow of which was mistaken at first for the galre of burning incendiary bombs.   Most of the damage done in Liverpool was due to unexploded A.A. shells, some of which fell in the National and Provincial Bank Bldgs, Water St,; Hale Rd; Banks Rd Recreation Ground; and Reynolds Park, Woolton.   Guinness' shed at Salthouse Dock was wrecked, one man being killed and others injured, and the shed floor flooded with the contents of stout barrels.   A fire watcher at Rank's Bldgs, Brunswick St, was also injured. A plane was shot down at Woore, Salop, two of 1 crew being killed & 3 others rounded up by Home Guards

MONTH OF OCTOBER ⇥ CONTD

OCTOBER 31:   The month ended with the first daylight alert
for several months and it ixx was in operation for about an hour.
In view of our experiences last year when a daylight "visitor"
usually presaged a night raid, people were not too happy and
in the evening as zero hour -- 8p.m to 9p.m at this time of the
year -- approached bus and tram drivers stood not upon the order of thei
thxiz their going but collected passenegrs as quickly as possible and
left the city x behind as soon as they could.   There was no raid,
however, and there were no incidents during the daylight alert.

ABOVE: The force of one bomb put a car in in to the front of this house in Brougham Road, Seacombe.

PERIOD OCTOBER TO MID FEBRUARY XX 1942. written 4th Feby, 1942.

The winter passed off amazingly quietly -- far more so than the great majority expected. Week after week passed without a sound of the siren. On x faty Nov 2nd/ 1941 activity was mainly on the Cheshire side of the river. Nine houses were partly demolished at the rear of Town Lane, BEBINGTON, and three people killed. Other bombs dropped at Malpas Drive, Hr Bebington; Bertram Drive, Meols; Pool Bank, Port Sunlight; Cornish Rd, Port Sunlight ; Garner St, Little Sutto and at Wallasey there were incidents at Grove Rd, Beverley Rd and Vyner Rd, whre two people were killed. Some bombs dropped on t shore at Hoylake where there was slight damage to the promenade. The only bomb dropped on the L'ppol side o the river was one at Croxteth Hall, where one dropped in a plantation without doing any damage.

The only other raid, up to February 4th, was on January 1@ when three bombs were dropped on the Liverpool side o t river, apparently by a harrassed raider. All fell in the Upper Stanhope St area, wherexx they damaged St Margaret's Church, Princes Rd, and damaged a number of houses in the Stanhope St area. Considering the few bombs dropped here the death roll was high at lea t fifteen being killed, many of them coloured people, and several others injured and trapped. For the first time since the war began -- but not for want of trying -- Jerry hit the oil installations at Ellesmere Port, although damage was slight and there was only one casualty$\frac{1}{2}$ Others dropped at Greasby (casualties two cows) and others harmlessly at in fields at Willaston.

ABOVE: Warning to the man who threatened Merseyside and the whole world.

*ABOVE: A mine causes havoc
near Everton Valley*

*ABOVE: A bath hangs perilously in position
in this bombed house.*

*ABOVE: A bobby on duty close
to where a parachute mine
devastated County Road.*

LEFT: How do you begin to deal with such damage?

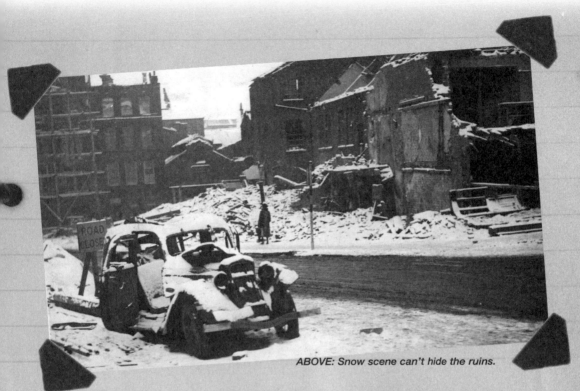

ABOVE: Snow scene can't hide the ruins.

*ABOVE: Total wreckage, but the Everton
Water Tower sits proudly on the horizon.*

ABOVE: City centre chaos.

*ABOVE: Bomb damage in
Lord Street in the city centre
in 1941.*

*ABOVE: Cracks suggest this
building is about to crumble.*

ABOVE: The famous St. Luke's Church at the top of Bold Street.

ABOVE: Fire watchers go
through their drill at Everton
Terrace ARP School.

ABOVE: Members of
the Merseyside
Home Guard in
special training.

ABOVE: Like a scene from the end of the world. The city centre took a real hammering.

ABOVE: A photograph of Liverpool's streets taken by the Luftwaffe.

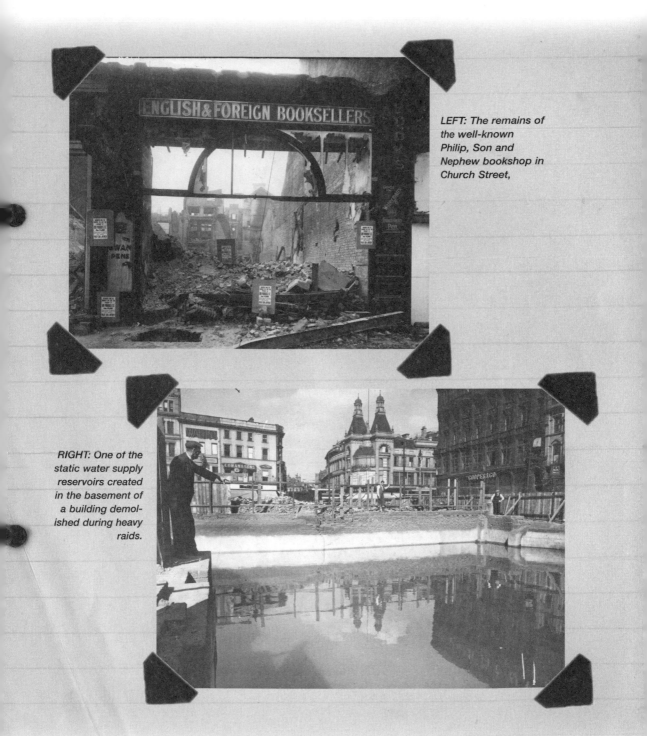

LEFT: The remains of the well-known Philip, Son and Nephew bookshop in Church Street,

RIGHT: One of the static water supply reservoirs created in the basement of a building demolished during heavy raids.

RIGHT: Working class dwellings damaged by German bombs in the Langrove Street/Great Homer Street area.

ABOVE: The Queen
Victoria Momument
stands gaunt
against a skyline of
destruction in 1940.

LEFT: The irony of three gable end
walls standing like monuments to the
houses they were once part of in
Ardleigh Road.